MW01059550

APOCALYPSE
HOW

LYPSE

OW

TURNING THE END TIMES INTO THE BEST OF TIMES

BY ROB KUTNER

RUNNING PRESS
PHILADELPHIA · LONDON

DEDICATION

To Sheryl, without whom my own world would end

ACKNOWLEDGEMENTS

Special thanks go to all of the following, who have earned a place in my underground compound: Talia Cohen at Laura Dail Literary Agency, Scott Sonneborn, Jacob Sager Weinstein, Steve and Jeanney Kutner, Ruthie Ellenson, Matthew Brozik, Maria Hjelm, Cathryn Michon, W. Bruce Cameron, Adam Thornton, and Mark Zohn.

© 2008 by Rob Kutner
All rights reserved under the Pan-American and
International Copyright Conventions

Printed in China.

*This book may not be reproduced in whole or in
part, in any form or by any means, electronic or
mechanical, including photocopying, recording, or
by any information storage and retrieval system
now known or hereafter invented, without written
permission from the publisher.*

9   8   7   6   5   4   3   2
Digit on the right indicates the number of this printing
Library of Congress Control Number: 2007932922

ISBN 978-0-7624-3233-2

This book may be ordered by mail from the publisher.
Please include $2.50 for postage and handling.
But try your bookstore first!

Running Press Book Publishers
2300 Chestnut Street
Philadelphia, PA 19103-4371

Visit us on the web!
www.runningpress.com

ART & DESIGN

Illustrations & photography by Joshua McDonnell except where noted.

Design by Joshua McDonnell
with assistance by Jason Kayser & Ryan Hayes.

Illustration:

Cover:
Mario Zucca (cow & surgical mask)
Jason Kayser (woman's face)
Jason Kernevich (skull)

Interior:
Mario Zucca pp. 13, 33, 34, 35, 40, 49, 51 (five 'hot spots'); 59, 71, 77, 89, 90-91, 96, 103-104, 122, 124-125, 138, 154-155, 168, 170, 180-181
Teresa Bonaddino p. 20
Matt & Gina p. 21
Jason Kayser pp. 38-39, 110-111, 119, 121, 126, 127, 166
Martha Rich pp. 80-81
Ryan Hayes p. 87
Jason Kernevich: All the 'Before We Blow' spreads.

© iStockphoto.com:
aleksandarvelasevic p. 51 (car); Mr_Vector p. 61 (wallpaper pattern);
Filo p. 106; Zuki p. 175;

Photography:

© iStockphoto.com:
blackred p. 2; matejmm p. 11; Juanmonino p. 26; Spauln p. 32; JLGutier-rez p. 44; photomorphic p 48; Redemption p. 54 (UFO); DNY59 p. 58; ImagineGolf p. 60; walrusmail p. 61; skodonnell p. 62; NickS p. 62; lsgaby p. 63; merlion p. 72; Mummu Media p. 78; Mienny p. 78; JJRD p. 78; kevinruss p. 78; Pkruger p. 94; garycookson p. 95; motoed p. 102; peepo p. 102;   jpa1999 p. 105 (metal); ene p. 105 (plate); jaroon p. 113; milosluz p. 116; jtyler p. 132, 164; RyanScott71 p. 136; spyChrome p. 138; Hogie p. 146; suprun p. 150; lobaaaato p. 152; dannyfroese p. 161; StanRohrer p. 165; dem10 p. 170;

Typography: Akzidenz Grotesk, Bookman, Cooper,

CONTENTS

FOREWORD by NOSTRADAMUS

When the Moon moves past the Seventh House
And Jupiter collides with Mars,
Then woe betide the planet Earth,
As mankind goeth the way of dinosaurs.

Continents raging, then subsiding,
Panic great consumes our species,
Chaos and terror rule the streets;
Undergarments fill with feces.

Lost as Theseus in his maze,
We see no sun from any latitude,
Tuesday indistinct from Thursday,
Friday earns the gods no gratitude.

But let not my prophecies excessively bum thee
out.

  For...

From the isle between the Hudson and the East
Comes forth a man with quill and vision deep;
His words sing wisdom for the darkening times,
His whimsy calms the ones who fail to sleep.

His book a beacon of advice
And lore not seen in all my prophecy,
With wondrous pictures, charts, and points of bullets,
For those whom Fate has struck with ADD.

Some shall sail through't like Jason on the Argo;
Some in bites, at lackadais'cal pace.
Some shall stow it in a berth of honor,
Some within their glowing fireplace.

And when the tribulation days arrive
For cities, nations, villages, and homes
Scores will howl, thousands more will scream
With laughter, as they face it with this tome—

Ah, confound these miserable confining quatrains...
I may have prophesied the Great Fire of London, the
French Revolution, Hitler, Hiroshima, the moon landings,
and the death of Princess Diana—but I could never have
foreseen the rise of a book like Apocalypse How.
    Read it, and Nostradamus' prediction?
    Laughter.

Michel de Nostredame
July, 1566 Saint-Remy-de-Provence

INTRODUCTION

"It's the end of the world as we know it/And I feel fine." —R.E.M.

LET'S FACE IT:
EVERYTHING ENDS

A beloved novel or TV series reaches its final moments. A night of blissful romance gives way to marriage. Even an everlasting gobstopper eventually loses all power to stop gobs.

So why should the world be any different?

As long as we humans have sought to make sense of the world, we have fretted over its demise. And honestly, where has that gotten us? One minute closer to that heart-stopping, civilization-melting, diet-and-lifestyle-modifying day—and no better prepared for it.

This is where *Apocalypse How* comes in.

In the pages of this book, you will learn so much about how to prepare for, survive, and adapt after any worldwide calamity, you will actually start to look forward to it. Your attitude will shift from "Oh God, we're screwed!" to "Bring it on, Jesus/Terrorists/Telekinetic Snail People from Alpha Centauri/Belgium![1]"

If you take away only one thing from this book, it's this: The world coming to an end isn't the end of the world.

And if it already has ended, you can also take a few pages out for kindling. You could roast a small pigeon over Chapter 6 alone.[2]

---

1 This book prepares you for all scenarios. That's just how good it is.

2 Not recommended if the world ends because of bird flu.

ARMAGEDDON:
THE BRIGHT SIDES!

Sure a world-ending war, natural disaster, or unforeseen cosmic event will mean incalculable destruction, the deaths of millions if not billions, and the possible poisoning of the earth for generations.

But if you are one of the lucky few to crawl out of the rubble,

you have **two** options:

Get mired in negativity.	**Choose to live by this simple but powerful credo:**
Oh boo hoo hoo. I can't find my family, or my left arm.	*When life gives you radioactive lemons, use a lead-shielded catapult to launch them at the foragers attacking your compound.*
Golly-gee willikers, my life would be so much easier if only we had electricity, the rule of law, or potable water.	
You can lie around bellyaching on top of what used to be your psychiatrists' office for days, weeks, months—until our simian overlords seize you as slave labor to build their fearsome, fourteen-story banana factory.	Stop focusing on everything we as a species have lost, and start appreciating everything you as an individual have gained. Namely: **time.** ——————→

You're familiar, no doubt, with the expression "all the time in the world." Well, that's nothing compared with all the time after it.

It starts when you open your eyes in the morning. Maybe you're awakened by the sounds of random gunfire, or the howling of souls being cast into the lake of fire. But at least it's not that godawful clock radio buzzer.

- Imagine the luxury of being able to return to a "snoozing" state as many times as you want—for intervals longer than nine minutes.

- And that's only the beginning. There's no morning train to miss, and the roads? Mile after mile of charred, twisted, skeleton-occupied hunks of metal. Talk about taking the guesswork out of traffic!

- Want to take a coffee[3] break? Take two, three, fifteen. Hang out as long as you want at the Spirit Bucket[4] with any surviving co-workers, gossiping about what the storytellers were chanting last night, or who mated with whom.

- Envision a world in which any second of the day that you choose is "quittin' time."

- None of which is to say you're even required to go to work anymore. Frankly, your office is more likely to be occupied by bloodthirsty gangs of wild-eyed orphans than passive-aggressive Betty from HR.

- As for your afternoons and evenings, they are now endless stretches of infinity, uncluttered by soccer practice, harp recitals, or tedious cocktail parties. Savor that last poorly reheated canapé: its memory will have to last you for eternity.

- And when night falls, all bets are off. Nothing to wake up for in the morning, no early store-closings or last calls at bars to contend with, no curfew. Except, perhaps, for the one imposed by the Robots.

- You don't just have time in a bottle; you've got an entire Spirit Bucket full of it. The question is, what are you going to do with it?

NO MORE WORLD = NO MORE...

DENTAL APPOINTMENTS • REALITY TV • CAR ALARMS • PARENT-TEACHER CONFERENCES
JUNK MAIL • 9-HOUR CABLE GUY REPAIR WINDOWS • TALKATIVE AIRPLANE SEATMATES
PARALLEL PARKING • BASEBALL RAIN DELAYS • COMPUTER VIRUSES • TOYOTATHONS
BLIND DATES • SPAM (EITHER KIND) • OBNOXIOUS CELLPHONE RINGTONES

---

3 Strictly speaking, probably some mixture of mud, water, and non-dairy creamer. But still, the best part of the day!
4 What future, ignorant generations will dub the water cooler.

OPPORTUNITIES

Have you ever wanted to travel the world? Now your world has effectively been reduced to a 500-square-mile radius of safe passage–done!

Ever dreamed of being #1 in the world at something? Downhill skiing, chess, World's Best Grandma, Best Supporting Actor in a Prime-Time Comedy Series? Good news, friend: The herd has been thinned. This is your moment to shine.[5]

How about learning that foreign language you've always wanted to? Mastering a musical instrument? Finally sitting down to tackle those big books you've always wanted to read?[6]

Or maybe you've been tempted to just chuck it all away and retire to grow organic vegetables. Now you may not have a choice.

What if you're just tired of who you are? Global meltdown is the ultimate clean slate. Reinvent yourself! Say goodbye to "Bert the Mid-Level Medical Supply Sales Rep" and hello to "Ragnar the Insurmountable."

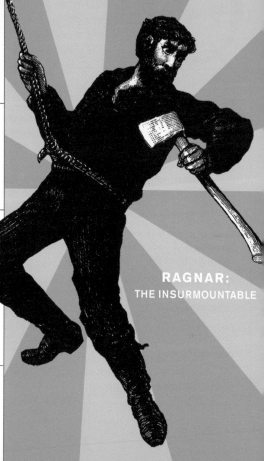

RAGNAR:
THE INSURMOUNTABLE

TO THE EXTENT THAT YOU CAN SEE ANY OF IT THROUGH THE PERMANENT CLOUD OF DUST AND ASH, THE SKY'S THE LIMIT.

[5] Especially in the wake of a nuclear holocaust.

[6] Which can be doubly useful in tackling anyone who tries to attack during "reading time."

BANG or WHIMPER

HOW
WE'RE GOING TO GO

Now that you're properly stoked for catastrophe (what motivational experts call the "Attitude of Splatitude"), you may be wondering: *So, how's it going to happen?*

Well, that's a matter of vigorous debate. However, the eschatologists here at Apocalypse How Laboratories offer you what we consider **the nine most likely scenarios.** ....◐

HOW WE'RE GOING TO GO

NUCLEAR BOMB

Mushroom clouds. Major cities microwaved. Poisoned air, water, and soil. Proud parents bragging what percentile their babies' tails are. A nuclear holocaust was an–all-too-familiar prospect during the Cold War.[7] Nowadays, it's highly improbable - requiring a cash-strapped former or wannabe superpower with stockpiles of nukes to somehow cross paths with suicidal zealots longing to radically remake the world. Save this one for the science fiction section, Mister.

ALIEN INVASION

Our water. Our labor. Our flesh. The Earth is such a smorgasboard for extraterrestrials, it's only a matter of time before they drop in for a bite. Assuming we don't defeat them via some ridiculously basic poison that their super-advanced science somehow failed to anticipate,[8] we could end up subletting our own planet from the worst slumlords ever.

RISE OF THE MACHINES

Think twice next time before you call your toaster a "two-slotted whore of Satan."[9] Our mechanical devices are getting smarter every day, and frankly, tired of our crap.[10] Sooner or later they're going to rise up, band together, and go haywire all over their masters. Worst of all, you just know this will happen the day after their warranties expire.

ASTEROID

Bright blue and green, our planet hangs out there in the universe like a huge beckoning target for some hotshot runaway rock. The last one of these big daddies wiped out the dinosaurs and froze the planet for millennia. In other words, if this global warming trend is for real, let's pick up the pace, people!

---

[7] Except to the small but fervent group known as "Nuclear Holocaust Deniers."

[8] "The color pink – it's deadly to them! Prepare the bubblegum cannon!"

[9] In our defense, do you think quality raisin bread just grows on trees?

[10] In particular, DX-9, the Hyper-Intelligent Commode.

ECOLOGICAL CATASTROPHE

Okay, maybe that last suggestion was a little hasty. If we keep consuming resources and polluting at the current rate, we're going to turn the Earth into one huge desert. Imagine an entire planet with all the ambience of the Middle East, but none of the oil. On the other hand, once the aliens get here, we can laugh our asses off at them.

NEUTRON BOMB

Millions of humans are killed, but infrastructures remain intact. Basically, the fantasy enjoyed daily by residents of Los Angeles and Tokyo.

EPIDEMIC

It starts with a monkey catching a case of the sniffles. Within days, people's insides are turning to jelly amidst the tragic sound of their last, useless words: "Wait, is it 'Starve an Ebola—Feed a Bird Flu,' or vice-versa…?"

MAD GENIUS' EVIL SCHEME

It could be anything, really: A photon cannon capable of blowing up the sun. A giant magnifying glass designed to boil away the oceans. A massive swarm of nuclear-reactor-wall-eating moths. Whatever fiendish plan this misunderstood brainiac with father issues undertakes, we can be sure of one thing: he will explain it in full to our hero, shackled helplessly in the madman's lair. Only, one of these days our hero is *not* going to escape, and *is* going to get eaten by sharks or sliced by a laser, testicles first. It's just the law of averages.

THE CHRISTIANS ARE RIGHT

More than one-quarter of the Bible is devoted to end-time prophecies, no more so than in the *Book of Revelation*.[11] According to its account, the end of the world will begin with the righteous being "Raptured"—directly lifted out of their clothes, jobs, cars, etc. to Heaven. There, they will have ringside seats (the ultimate Skybox) to watch everyone else "left behind" (Jews, Muslims, atheists, the wrong kinds of Christians, et al.) undergo: 1,000 years of torment and tribulation by the minions of Antichrist, sixteen airport-bookstore novels written about them, and eventually, the return of Jesus for the ultimate grudge match. (**SPOILER ALERT:** Jesus wins.)

[11] Cf. Bible, the end.

OTHER RELIGIONS' BELIEFS ABOUT THE END

JUDAISM—The exiles will be gathered to Israel, the dead resurrected, and all humanity will live in a redeemed world. For sinners, not so much an eternity in Hell as an eternal sense of guilt.

HINDUISM—According to the *Markandeya Purana*, the world will be ended by the *Pralay* (literally, "destruction"), an all-destroying flood. Small wonder the religion prizes not only piety, but absorbency.

HOPI—This Native American nation believes the land will be covered in iron snakes, stone rivers, and a giant spider's web; the seas will turn black, and a huge blue star will crash into the Earth. This is believed to be the only eschatology invented by a six-year-old boy.

BUDDHISM—Buddha's teachings will disappear from the Earth, only to be reinstated by a new Buddha. Unsurprisingly, the "mellowest" of the end-time scenarios.

MORMONISM—Jesus Christ will return to Earth at Jackson County, Missouri, where he will miraculously turn corn into corn dogs and water into ginger ale. OK, that might not be exactly it—we were too busy slamming the door into the face of the guy telling us about it.

ISLAM—A grand judgment for all, during which believers are distinguished from infidels by producing more sweat, but are eventually given a sweet drink that abolishes thirst eternally. Hard to believe they came up with this in the desert.

NORSE MYTHOLOGY— A cataclysmic, all-destroying battle between the gods, known as Ragnarok—whose name shall inspire countless garage bands and teenage boy locker inscriptions.

MAYAN—The famously sophisticated Mayan calendar predicted a "great change" would occur in our year 2012, which some interpret as a reference to the end. Isn't it funny how you can be good at predicting the end of someone *else's* civilization, but….

ZOROASTRIANISM—The Earth will be devoured by fire, after which sinners will be punished for three days, then forgiven. Come on, 72 hours? We've had hangovers that lasted longer.

WHAT TO EXPECT WHEN WE'RE EXPLODING

Briefly, and in no particular order:
- mass confusion and terror
- anarchy
- a sudden, worldwide explosion of armpit moisture

Don't be one of the panicking billions. Instead,
FOLLOW OUR EXCLUSIVE

THREE-STEP PLAN TO A BRIGHTER DOOMSDAY™[12]

STEP 1

KEEP A COOL HEAD
BELOW ARE THREE EXAMPLES OF POSSIBLE REACTIONS YOU CAN HAVE:

PERSON A
"I'm terrified, but keeping it together."

PERSON B
"I'm going to be A-OK!"

PERSON C
"I'm probably not."

NOT TO SPEAK ILL OF THE DEAD, BUT PERSON C? DEFINITELY **NOT** A COOL HEAD.

[12] Copyright expires 75 years after the death of the author, or planet.

STEP 2

Conduct an Inventory of Yourself/Civilization

The number of working eyes/arms/legs I have is:

A. 1

B. 2

C. <1

The main color I see from my window is:

A. Glowing green

B. Metallic silver

C. Window?

Complete the following: My ____ is on fire.

A. House

B. Family

C. Spinal column

All around me, I hear:

A. People screaming and calling out for loved ones

B. Authority figures, urging calm

C. The voices of Grandma and the late Jimmy Stewart, calling me "home"

I have enough food and supplies to get me through:

A. 2-3 months

B. The Siege of Leningrad

C. Super Bowl Sunday

KEY: If you answered anything but "c" to any of those, you're going to be just fine. If you answered "c," you are almost certainly not reading this. (Though if somehow you are, could you get a copy of this to God? We would *love* a blurb from Him for the second edition.)

STEP 3

READ AND MEMORIZE
EVERY WORD OF THIS BOOK

THREE WAYS TO READ *APOCALYPSE HOW*

1. Before (recommended)
At the end of each chapter you'll find a section entitled "Before We Blow," chock full of tips, to-dos, and checklists to help you prepare for the Big Day.

2. During
Apocalypse How is a quick, easy-to-use reference guide, divided into topical chapters on Food & Supplies, Relocation, Clothing, Social Life, Fitness & Health, Recreation, and Career, Wealth & Power.

3. After
On the run from the Four Horsemen or an army of poisonous Robot Wasps (not recommended).

CHAPTER 1
FOOD & SUPPLIES

FOOD AND SUPPLIES: YOUR NEW BEST FRIENDS

"Hey Ma, what do we have to eat?"

An annoying question from a 19-year-old just back from college. A heart-breaking plea during the Great Depression. Immediate grounds for "turning this car around right now" on a road trip to Disney World.

But in the exciting, anything-goes afterworld, the answer is: an endless feast of options!

FAST FORAGE
REPLICATING THE AMERICAN DIET IN AN AGE OF LEAN

Let's begin with a little straight talk. In the post-apocalyptic age, we are not going to have access to the traditional American diet, which—according to the latest research—consists of:

Breakfast Two sausage links
Two strips bacon
9 pancakes
1-3 bowls Donut-Os: The Cereal Made of Actual Donuts
Chocolate-flavored orange juice
Donuts

Lunch One Pizza Cheeseburgerito Grande
One barrel Refried French Fries
Diet Coke
Donuts

Dinner 18-oz steak in hot dog gravy
7 scoops mashed potatoes with vegetable-colored specks (optional)
1.5 square inches iceberg lettuce, deep fried
Donut sundae

As well-equipped for survival as such meals leave us, in the coming era of more finite resources (and severely limited access to FryDaddies), we will need new, creative ways to recapture our glorious culinary past.

How do we do that? Let's look at the basics.

MEAT:
SOON, MORE THAN EVER

Even in a world potentially wracked by disease, Martians, or the Hordes of Satan, mammals will abound, their soft (or softenable) parts just ours for the chomping. But in order to fully enjoy this "all-you-can-find" buffet, a few preconceptions need to be addressed.

It's Not "Road Kill," It's "Slow-Moving Delicacies"

Think of your favorite short-order diner or beachside stand, where the freshest creatures are slapped right on a hot grill, seared to perfection, and dished up to you with a squeeze of lemon.

Now consider this: There are over four million miles of asphalted road lining the United States alone. In the absence of automobile traffic bound to accompany our society's shutdown, that's like one humongous two-billion-foot-long grill, but with
- NO waiting and
- NO "Chatty Cathy" waitress to tip

You will have to supply your own lemon, though. Sorry, you're just going to have to get used to roughing it sooner or later.

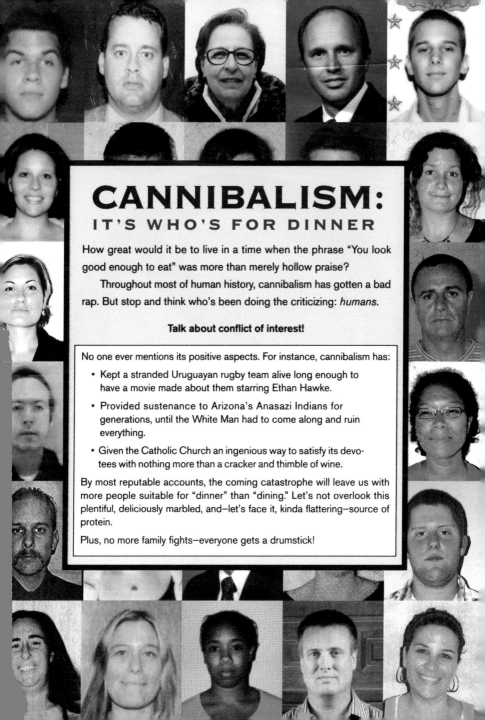

CANNIBALISM:
IT'S WHO'S FOR DINNER

How great would it be to live in a time when the phrase "You look good enough to eat" was more than merely hollow praise?

Throughout most of human history, cannibalism has gotten a bad rap. But stop and think who's been doing the criticizing: *humans.*

Talk about conflict of interest!

No one ever mentions its positive aspects. For instance, cannibalism has:

- Kept a stranded Uruguayan rugby team alive long enough to have a movie made about them starring Ethan Hawke.
- Provided sustenance to Arizona's Anasazi Indians for generations, until the White Man had to come along and ruin everything.
- Given the Catholic Church an ingenious way to satisfy its devotees with nothing more than a cracker and thimble of wine.

By most reputable accounts, the coming catastrophe will leave us with more people suitable for "dinner" than "dining." Let's not overlook this plentiful, deliciously marbled, and—let's face it, kinda flattering—source of protein.

Plus, no more family fights—everyone gets a drumstick!

•BREAD•

THE THING MAN DOES NOT LIVE BY ALONE

Throughout human history, bread has had a hallowed place in our lives and cultures, serving two critical purposes:

1. **KEEPING MEAT FROM STAINING OUR FINGERS**
2. **WHAT YOU EAT WHEN YOU CAN'T GET MEAT**

But is bread more trouble than it's worth in a post-catastrophic world? Consider all the steps required to make this "dietary diva":

① GROWING THE GRAIN

② HARVESTING THE GRAIN

③ GRINDING THE GRAIN

④ REFINING THE FLOUR

⑤ OBTAINING YEAST

⑥ MAKING THE DOUGH

⑦ FILLING IT WITH ONLY THE PLUMPEST MALAGA RAISINS AND CHOICEST CEYLON CINNAMON[13]

⑧ KNEADING THE DOUGH

⑨ WAITING FOR IT TO RISE

⑩ BAKING IT

All that for a dull, dry foodstuff that, within two days, is all but inedible. What we're saying is, leave the bread to the roving bands of feral hippies, and focus on the bounteous assortment of other foods that the Lord (and the wreckage of human civilization) have placed before you.

The test chefs at Apocalypse How Kitchens have come up with the following fun, fast, and *extremely* creative recipes for post-apocalyptic dining:

13 If you want us to eat it, that is.

THE DIET AFTER

TEN RECIPES FOR THE END OF THE WORLD

Tumbleweed Surprise

2-3 MEDIUM TUMBLEWEEDS, FRESHLY ROLLED-INTO-TOWN

1 CAN CAMPBELL'S CREAM OF MUSHROOM SOUP, LOOTED

1 CUP CRUSHED GLASS

Mix well and pour into bowls. The next time your family/clan/polygamistic-compound complains, "Oh no, tumbleweed *again?*" just tell them to take a bite... then yell, "Surprise!"

Leatherguini Alfredo

36 INCHES OF LEATHER FROM A SHOE, JACKET, OR MARITAL AID, CUT INTO ½ INCH STRIPS

WATER

WHITE POWDER OF YOUR CHOICE[14]

Soak leather (or boil, if you're feeling gourmet) until non-tooth destroying. Mix with water and powder, and enjoy!

Steve Tartare

1 RECENTLY PERISHED BODY, MALE

Check for signs of radiation or disease. And also his wallet. Is his name Steve? It is now. Serve at cave temperature with a garnish of Phyllis.

[14] With a dish like this, it's really more about presentation.

Stone Soup

1 Fresh Stone

Yes, that beloved children's story was not really a parable about cooperation. It was an encoded survival manual. Many people are skeptical of this one, but take it from us: the secret is a fresh, high-quality stone. Don't just cut corners and throw in a cheap piece of igneous. Splurge on a sedimentary—because *you're worth it.*

Moo Shu Varmint

1 cup "flour"

1 cup water, non-toxic

two tablespoons Hoisin sauce[15]

1 varmint[16]

Mix flour and water and roll into a pancake. You remember, just like Mom used to make you on Sundays before going to church. Until you found an empty pile of her clothes next to a smoking griddle. Now she's making pancakes for Jesus (assuming he's not diabetic).

Soylent Brown

1 lb. finely minced PEOPLE!

1 tsp. powdered PEOPLE!

Salt, to taste

Combine and roast in a human brain-pan over a low fire of human bones (try the tibia for a hint of "legginess") until Hispanic or lightly African-American.[17] Placates 2-4 alien masters for, like, a minute.

---

[15] Yes, we realize such things are tough to come by, but honestly–it's just not Moo Shu without the hoisin.

[16] We recommend one of the more succulent Dadgum or Cotton-Pickin' varieties.

[17] Unless you've just chopped up and roasted a Hispanic or African-American, in which case, RACIST!

Self-Microwaving Popcorn

1 IRRADIATED CORNFIELD

One of the many perks of a nuclear holocaust, this snack couldn't be easier. Find an irradiated cornfield, making sure to steer clear of the typical dangers (alien landing pads, demon children, baseball player ghosts), and pick away to your heart's content. If you're jonesing for "movie popcorn" butter, check the remains of your local multiplex—that substance has almost certainly survived intact.

Stunted Leg of Lamb

4 LAMBS, MUTATED[18]

MINT JELLY/RADIOACTIVE SLUDGE

1 SPRIG FRESH ROSEMARY/
BELLY BUTTON LINT

Clearly, this recipe is friendly to substitutions. But don't skimp on the lamb. If you try and just cut down a normal leg, you'll get that unpleasant "healthy DNA" aftertaste.

Ash Browns

ONE SURFACE OF ANY STILL-STANDING
STRUCTURE

ONE SQUEEGEE

Love sno-cones, but can't wait until nuclear winter? Put your mouth right up to the surface, scrape, and enjoy!

Giant Cockroach Au Vin

5 LBS. COCKROACHES,
DE-EXOSKELETONED

3 CUPS HOME-BREWED WINE (TRY A FULL-
BODIED RAISIN, DANDELION, OR MAYBE A
LATE-SEASON FUNGUS)

2 TBS. FINES HERBES[19]

The beauty of this recipe is that you can find the ingredients no matter what happens to the Earth. Heat until cockroaches are tender, or if no heating source is available, drink wine, close eyes, and imagine pretzels.

---

[18] Unless you can find one lamb with all four legs stunted. But come on—no one's *that* lucky.

[19] May also substitute a handful of weeds, squished.

Special OCCASIONS

What about those times when the usual run-of-the-mill fare just won't suffice? How do you properly celebrate life's newest most precious moments? A territory-consolidating marriage. The birth of your first mutant child. A "Bot Mitzvah."[20]

Here's a few considerations for "breaking out the good stuff."

Check the vintage
Many pre-apocalyptic packaged foods contain a "sell by" or "enjoy by" date. Just think how much more you can enjoy these "finely aged delectables" now.

Color Schemes
Does your canned food still have its labels? Mix and match a green[21] with a red, a yellow with a purple. Is it unlabelled? Then your celebration is doubled into a surprise party!

Powdered to the People
Always keep some powdered milk in reserve for guests. Sure, you could attempt to force milk out of that mule or bondwoman in your yard, but it just won't have that "factory-desiccated" taste.

---

[20] That special day when your cyborg offspring stands up and declares "Today I am half a man."

[21] However, we would not recommend displaying any labels showing large green giants if there are actual ones around.

THE HUNT IS ON.

Soylent Green. Omega Man. Planet of the Apes.

There's a reason Charlton Heston has starred in so many classics of apocalyptiana, and it's not just because his acting style is best described as "yelling like it's the end of the world."

One of the many groups most eagerly awaiting the apocalypse is the organization he led, the National Rifle Association. And no wonder. A world without laws means no gun control, and a hunting season that's year-round (to the extent there are seasons anymore).

Whether you like guns, or just eating, the post-Armageddon era provides a boundless set of opportunities for hunting. Among them:

Endangered Species: Technically, a term that now applies to every species, especially your own. But in practical terms, this is your chance to match wits with the peripheral vision of the Spotted Owl, take on the speed challenge of a Caribou, or learn what a Bald Eagle tastes like (our guess: freedom).

No Bag Limits: …other than the number of bags you and your slaves can haul. The only kind of "poaching" you can be accused of in the coming world is deliciously cooking your catch with a small amount of water.

Choose Your Weapon: Rifles, shotguns, and bows-and-arrows. Until now, those were the only legally recognized options. But haven't you ever wondered what it would be like to down a whitetail deer with a ninja throwing star? A mallard with a bowling pin? A bobcat with another bobcat? Go for it! Remember: If you can dream it, you can kill it…with it.

Becoming the Hunted: Be honest: You've always enjoyed the cat-and-mouse aspect of hunting, but felt limited by having to be on the "trigger" end of the gun. Now that you're fair game, let the games begin!

You may be familiar with the expression "You are what you eat." Well, that's all fine and dandy for a society obsessed with things like "diet" and "meals" and "nutrients." But in the afterworld, the more useful formulation is going to be "You are *where* you eat"—or more precisely, "Where you eat, you are."

The exciting part is, this means that the quest for nourishment can also become a journey of self-discovery. Will you be just another member of the herd, picking over the obvious (and frankly, boring!) remains of the supermarkets, restaurants, and warehouses? Or will you strike out and express your individuality by noshing in unexpected places?

If you do want to stay far from the madding crowd (particularly as famine makes them even "maddinger"), we recommend the following unconventional sites for **FUN FOOD FINDS:**

Zoos

Obviously, this will be an early target for the oh-so-trendy *hungerati*. You're not going to get the fresh zebra or, honestly, even the pick of the snakes. But remember what else a decimated zoo contains: tons of feed, and no one to dispense it. Anyone can eat plain old human food—tonight, you're *dining like a lemur.*

Kindergartens

After the elementary, junior, and senior high school cafeterias have been ravaged, and the "shoestring fry" stops being a unit of currency, seek out these hidden repositories of sugary goodness. Every pre-school teacher worth her temporary state certification has stashed countless tons of bribe-candy, gallons of apple juice, and square-feet of graham cracker against a six-year-old insurgency.

YOUR TAKEOUT

Sports Venues

Once the refugees realize the government is never coming and disperse from here, you move in. Sure, they've emptied out the concession stands, but you've got tens of thousands of seat-bottom smorgasboards to dine off of. As you enjoy your "chewable feast," remember to thank the hyperactive brat who stuck it there during a boring sixth inning.

Natural History Museums

You've always had a soft spot for crispy duck. How about a turkey that already comes pre-stuffed? And if you're dining "a la cave," why not surprise the clan by dragging home an actual mastodon? Arrange entire meals around a theme: one night make it Mesozoic; the next, Aztec. They're certainly what they would have eaten.

Las Vegas

Even after its casinos dim and its last showgirls lower their legs, this desert hotspot will continue to enjoy the actual but little-known phenomenon behind its success: its miraculous all-you-can-eat-buffet springs. Those who make it past the fearsome, reanimated Golden Nugget Cowboy are in for an endless supply of spontaneously generated day-old shrimp cocktails and rubbery steaks.

Marketing Firms

Imagine: thousands of potentially bestselling test products, and barely enough people left on Earth to form a focus group. That is, until *you* step over the shards of what used to be the one-way mirror. Dine to your heart (and demographic consumer preference)'s content on the world's last—and only—supply of everything from Gravy Balls to Sour Cream n' Onion Soda.

Imagine No Possessions...

Fortunately, you won't have to.
Even in the wake of a collapsed industrial economy, there is still
a cornucopia of wondrous treasures out there for the taking.

••

Don't believe us? It's been proven in the cutting-edge field known as
Aftermathematics

According to the Havingstuff Ratio:
H (the amount of stuff you can have)

$$H = \frac{\textbf{Possessions}}{\textbf{Possessors}}$$

After an earth-shattering event, that formula changes to:

$$H = \frac{\textbf{Possessions}}{\text{💀 💀 💀 💀 💀}}$$

Since Aftermathematics allows us to divide by "dead guy skulls," the result is:

$$\textbf{H = 1 shitload}^{[22]}$$

In other words, when nearly everyone else goes away, the world
becomes your personal garage sale–minus the ceramic gnomes and
three-years-out-of-date "Dogs Dressed as People" calendars.

---

[22] According to Aftermathematics, a "shitload" will be a key post-apocalyptic unit of measurement.

CHECKLIST

STUFF OR CRAP? A Scientific Approach

In the post-apocalyptic world, The Rolling Stones are proven wrong[23]: You can always get you want. The problem is getting just what you need. To help you separate essential from non-, before you acquire a new item, make sure it meets the conditions outlined in the following checklist.

I can use this item to: __ cook

__ eat

__ hit someone whom I can then cook and eat

I can carry this item using my: __ arms

__ wheeled vehicle

__ pack of mongrel slaves

I can trade this item for: __ gasoline

__ food

__ five glorious minutes of someone scratching my sores

This item will likely last: __ indefinitely

__ until I can repair or trade it

__ at least until the Year 3

This item would be of great value to: __ the underground resistance

__ our new masters

__ that hottie whose loincloth I've been trying to get into

If the item doesn't meet any of those criteria, toss it. Let the next generation find it, puzzle over it, maybe start a religion around it. Suckers!

[23] In fact, Keith Richards will in all likelihood be around for you to tell to his face.

Stash and Carry

So now you've gone out and found, bartered, stolen, extorted, or guilt-tripped your way to a kingly stash. Unfortunately, in any end-of-the-world scenario, there are going to be some greedy gusses who just can't be satisfied with what they have. Meaning, you're going to have to hide your loot. Fortunately, storage space is one of the afterworld's most abundant natural resources.

Let's look at the different options for your items of choice:

On You

ARMPIT

Con: Will smell like armpit
Pro: Those with serious B.O. will have no fear of theft

HUNG AROUND NECK

Con: Strain on neck, back
Pro: Scares away superstitious hostiles who think it's your god

WAISTBAND

Con: May block attempts to repopulate
Pro: Depending on shape, may enhance invitations to repopulate

RECTUM

Con: May impair walking
Pro: May enhance walking

Around You

TREE
Pro: Hard for thieves to reach
Con: Easy for family of five living up there to break

BUSH
Pro: Good hiding place
Con: Great urinating place

UNDERGROUND
Pro: Safe, dry, secure
Con: Gives unfair advantage to pirates

WATER
Pro: Keeps it clean
Con: Hard to get to through cluster of corpses

AS A FURTHER GUIDE, HERE ARE A FEW SPECIFIC SUGGESTIONS ON

HOW TO DETER ANY APOCALYPTIC ENEMY FROM STEALING YOUR STASH

Sentient Machines

DETERRENT: Bucket full of water

EFFECT: Stirs up fears of rust, short-circuiting, fishing bait

Punk Biker Gang

DETERRENT: Scattering of nails

EFFECT: Double-scare: punctured tires, tetanus shots

Four Horsemen

DETERRENT: Pentagram

EFFECT: Suggests the disturbing presence of a local death metal band

Aliens

DETERRENT: Statue of Xlornanx holding up a Tjagu

EFFECT: Self-explanatory

Mutants

DETERRENT: A *Sports Illustrated* swimsuit Calendar, next to a mirror

EFFECT: Fills them with poor body image

A FINAL WORD

The post-apocalyptic period is a wonderful opportunity to practice the ancient Buddhist/poor person art of *simplicity*. After all these years of trying to keep up with the Joneses, now you can change your focus to keeping away from them. If you've got something you can't use or eat, don't be afraid to simply dump it, wherever you are. After all, it's not like you're going to pollute the Earth any further.

And if it helps, keep the following mantra in mind:
Nobody likes a packrat. Except when impaled on a stick and roasted.

BEFORE WE BLOW

YOUR ESSENTIAL TO-HOARD LIST (sponsored by Costco™)

FOOD
PERISHABLE Dried fruits (Best Sources: Hiking-supply stores, senior citizens' pantries)

NON-PERISHABLE Pre-packaged or simple preparations only (Chef Larousse's Easy-Broil Leek Souffle with a Balsamic Reduction and Elderberry Confit—not recommended[24])

MEDICINE
CONVENTIONAL Pain relievers and essential "antis" only: antiseptics, antibiotics, anti-inflammatories
(Less Essential: anti-depressants, anti-aging, antacids)

TRADITIONAL Chinese herbs, crystals, snake oil, virgin blood (Stock up—you'll make a killing in the new world)

FUEL

GASOLINE

BATTERIES

WOOD (Note: Wooden tchotchkes your parents brought you from their travels burn just as well, if not better)

SUNDRIES

CUTTING IMPLEMENTS

REPAIRING IMPLEMENTS

CUTTING-ANYONE-WHO-TRIES-TO-TAKE-YOUR-CUTTING-OR-REPAIRING-IMPLEMENTS IMPLEMENTS

[24] Pretty much applies to anything in the Chef Larousse line, with the exception of Chef Larousse's Baggie of Peanuts

CHAPTER 2

RELOCATION, RELOCATION, RELOCATION

Getting Away From It All

We're all looking for our place in the world. That's just the human condition. But when the human condition expands to include the seven-headed Whore of Babylon emerging from the sea, or an epidemic of toxic, self-imploding flatulence, we're going to have to look a lot faster.

But you, my friend, will be one step ahead of the terrified mobs, because this chapter will give you the tools you need to find, get to, and settle into your new place in the sun—even if an evil madman's device has sent our planet hurtling toward it.

First priority, though, is determining what end-time environs are best suited for you and your family/tribe/shiv-wielding outlaw band. Ask yourself the following questions:

- Am I more of an "indoors, crouched behind a barricade" or an "outdoors, dodging red-hot shards of cosmic rock" person?

- Do I envision myself running from uniformed apes on horseback through the streets of a city?

- Do I prefer a small town where everyone calls out my name, usually followed by "…is hoarding gasoline. Get 'im!"?

The *Apocalypse How* **fully interactive Flee-Chart,** found on the next two pages will help you pick the last locale that's right for you.

THE *APOCALYPSE HOW* FLEE-CHART

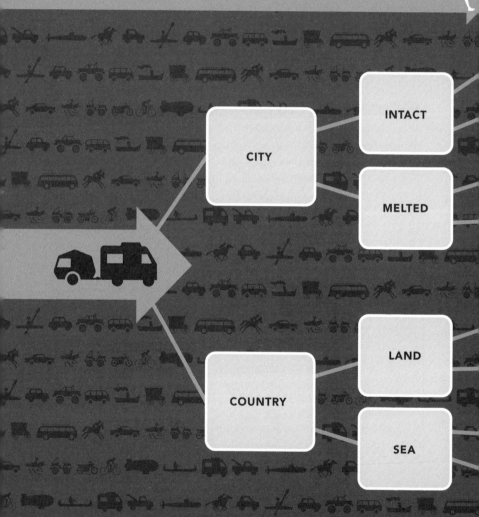

CITY

INTACT

MELTED

COUNTRY

LAND

SEA

46

SMALL TOWN	DODGE CITY, 2.0
NO LIGHTS, BIG CITY	VILLAGE OF THE DAMNED
URBAN JUNGLE	DETROIT
FASCIST DYSTOPIA	RESISTANCE HIDEOUT (SEWER)
DESERT	ROBOT/ALIEN LABOR CAMP
FOREST	GLASSED-OVER
MANMADE ARCHIPELAGO OF URINE-DRINKING MERCENARIES	FRESHLY CREATED
CRUISE SHIP	THUG-FILLED
	SMOLDERING

Hasty TRAVEL & LEISURE

M A G A Z I N E

TOP GETAWAYS FOR GETTING AWAY!

Still didn't find what you're looking for? Fortunately, there are a few places that are all but assured of safety and security from any manner of damage we or others inflict on the planet. And, thanks to their remoteness and relative inaccessibility, if you and yours can make it to one, you're guaranteed not to be followed by hordes of the "wannabe survivors" you'll find just about everywhere else.

1. Antarctica

Advantages: Securely remote location, boundless fowl and fish, world's biggest subzero freezer

Disadvantages: Permanent "shrinkage" = difficult repopulation

2. Top of K-2 (Pakistan)

Advantages: Clean mountain air, helpful sherpas

Disadvantages: Very thin clean mountain air, last days spent surrounded by Euro-backpackers

3. Next to Great Wall of China (China)

Advantages: Guaranteed protection from Mongols, Huns, Taiwanese

Disadvantages: One of those three bound to re-invent the pogo stick[26]

4. Atlantis (???)

Advantages: Wise and advanced civilization, shielded under miles of water from land-dwellers' follies

Disadvantages: May not exist

5. "It's a Small World" Ride, Disneyworld (USA)

Advantages: Complete impregnability, except to those wielding a "FastPass"

Disadvantage: Designed by Walt Disney to drive flesh-and-blood survivors to suicide with that damned song, clearing the way for his army of ethnically diverse automatons

---

25 Figure of speech only—in actual fact, these may be some of the few spots on the planet that are not hot.

26 Our money's on the Taiwanese.

Should I Stay or Should I Flee?

My house is now under _____.

A. martial law

B. constant watch by would-be looters

C. water

My last meal consisted of _____.

A. creatively used local foodstuffs (a la Chapter 1)

B. the morning distribution of "Humanoid Food Pellets"

C. my left arm

Despite current conditions, I am in communication with _____.

A. family members, friends, neighbors

B. our fearsome yet fair new rulers.

C. the restless voices of the damned

The first thing I do every morning is _____.

A. make sure my family and possessions are secure

B. ascend to the surface to look for survivors

C. try to determine if it's morning or evening

I hope my children grow up to be _____.

A. tribal leaders

B. members of the resistance

C. _____

KEY: If you answered "a" to all or most, you're sitting pretty right where you are. If you said "b" you're sitting unattractive-but-with-a-good-personality. If you said "c" keep reading...

KING OF THE ROAD

WHEN YOUR WAY IS THE HIGHWAY

Whether you know your ultimate destination, or just that it's *anywhere but where you currently are*, you're in for one of Armageddon's most exciting adventures. The lure of the open road! The scent of secure locations! The knowledge that every mile, every landmark, every rest-stop and scenic vista before you has been returned to a virgin frontier, with you as its Lewis and/or Clark.

It's no wonder the roads are certain to be clogged with thousands of your fellow thrill/refuge-seekers.

So how do you prepare for your "road-warrior trip?" It starts with what and how you pack. Here are a few must-grabs for the resourceful refugee:

 LUGGAGE As sturdy a backpack as you can find/loot. Although any top-notch retailer's wares will do, we recommend Land's End–they're the only one whose name accurately reflects the current situation. Coming in a distant second are rollerboards, those wheeled carry-on bags popular among airline travelers. While on the surface they seem more comfortable and convenient, those tiny wheels are likely to get gummed up with anything from radioactive ash to meteor dust to the remains of the faster but less fortunate.

 FOOD-DRYING EQUIPMENT Remember how we used to laugh at those late-night infomercials? You and your travel companions will be the only ones laughing now, when you're feasting on Rat Jerky.

 EMPTY CONTAINERS Potable water, fuel, semi-virgin olive oil. You're going to need liquids for survival, and more to the point, something to carry them in. Be creative! In this new, "anything goes" world, just about *anything* can be a container: from housepet skulls to hollowed-out plasma-screen TVs. Even that old condom in your wallet would be misused controlling births in this depopulated world. Fill 'er up, open wide, and enter the exciting world of the drug mule!

 WEAPONS The post-apocalyptic world is a weapon-lover's paradise. As we learned in Ch.1, guns can be acquired and used by anyone at any time–just like present-day America, but *without the waiting period!* Knives are no longer a source of bewilderment in your kitchen. When you're under attack by gas-hungry bikers, it doesn't matter if you slice, saw, debone, prune, or fillet them. As for the eternal classic, Things You Can Hit Other People With, there's no limit. Basically, anything non-fragile you're carrying will work.[27]

---

[27] If you are keeping anything fragile, please reconsider: those Hummel figurines are going to be worth something *no* day.

PLANNING YOUR TRIP

Getting Away from There is Half the Fun

Escaping a catastrophe is the great ender of male-female travel squabbles. There are no shortcuts, you probably don't want to stop and ask anyone, and there's pretty much no danger of having "gone too far."

Furthermore, mapping out your escape can be fun and easy, by contrast with past efforts. No more are you burdened with figuring out alternate, lower-traffic routes–there are none. Gone is the pressure of making a certain amount of miles toward a destination per day. Now, it's only a question of how many miles you can get from wherever you currently are. And forget about getting confused by all those small towns that aren't on the map. If things are bad enough to necessitate this journey, nothing will be on it.

In fact, it's no longer a map—it's a blank slate, yours for the re-imagining. Make it a family activity. Gather the kids/slaves/sentient-goats around, grab a magic marker/sharpened piece of coal/recently used dagger and re-draw your world! No more "Sioux Falls"—now it's "Supersonic Fairyland." Bye-bye "Rhode Island," hello "Republic of Irving!"

And when you leave, definitely bring that map with you, if for no other reason than to avoid going in circles. Make simple, easy-to-read markings to identify terrain as you're passing by: for instance, "G" for "Green Cloud of Gas," "Z" for "Zombie Army on the March," "F" for "Currently/Perpetually on Fire."

ARE WE SAFE YET?

REMAINS-OF-THE-ROAD TRIP GAMES FOR THE WHOLE FAMILY

The air is sweltering. Everyone's thirsty. The kids are screaming—no wait, actually, that's the parents. No matter. It's going to take a while to get away from wherever you're fleeing. And it's a little hard to make the "I'm going to turn this around right now" threat stick when there's an alien mothership hovering behind you.

Fortunately, escape can be a great time for family-bonding activities. Whether you're traveling with toddlers, teens, or shockwave-induced mental man-children, the following games should keep them diverted for hours.

"I Spy" Certainly you remember this one from childhood. What's particularly invigorating about the post-apocalyptic version, though, is a whole new range of previously unknown colors and spectacles ("I spy something GREEN…coming out of someone's head.") It's sure to keep the little ones guessing.

"License Plates" In a more peaceful world, if you played this one-note game long enough, all the plates seemed to hail from one city alone: Dullsville. But in the wake of massive destruction, the possibilities for plate variety are so much greater. How many mangled plates can your young ones spot? Charred? Being used to roast a human head over a nearby campfire?

"Former State Capitols" As noted above, the old geographic designations may no longer apply. But since those pieces of useless knowledge are still taking up space in our heads, why not make the most of them? Update this classic with a simple one-word substitution: "The capitol of North Dakota *was*…"

"Punch Buggy" Used to be, this was a pretty dull game. As exciting as the prospect of a parentally sanctioned blow on a sibling's arm was, did anyone ever spot a Volkswagen Beetle often enough to sustain interest? In the new pre-industrial era, however, *actual buggies* (of the horse-drawn type) will be so common, your kids will be black and blue in no time!

DON'T MISS THESE NEWLY CREATED
ROADSIDE ATTRACTIONS

No matter what part of the country you're leaving for another, an event of catastrophic significance is bound to alter the landscape, sometimes in the most picturesque ways. Here are a few highlights worth pausing from even the most panicky of flights for:

THE POPCORN PALACE

South Dakota's famous Corn Palace, as altered by explosion or fireball. Finally, a landmark with its own built-in snack bar!

THE WORLD'S BIGGEST BALL OF PLUTONIUM

While it's advised not to get too close to this one, the good news is, you can see it from several states away.

GRACELAND

A place of refuge attracting thousands seeking escape from the sad wreckage of their lives. In other words, exactly the same function it served before.

THE GRAND GLACIER

Bound to be the Neo Ice Age's most popular tourist destination. Though you do kind of have to feel sorry for the donkeys dispatched to take you into it.

MT. RUSH-EVEN-MORE

Thought it was impressive to see the monumental heads of four American presidents? How much more impressive will it be to see a mutated, *two*-headed Lincoln![28]

---

[28] We would not, of course, make the absurd claim that radioactivity could somehow cause mutations in mountainous rock. Rather, the second head will be added on by escaped mutants as a bold (if ultimately futile) cry for emancipation.

Re-Settling Down

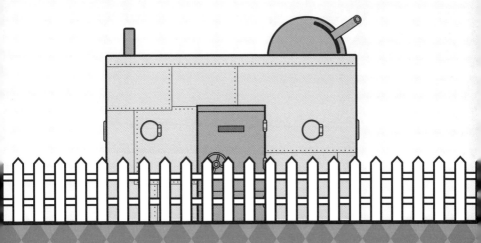

--------- **Making Your Hideout a Home** ---------

So you've gotten yourself and your companions away from danger—or at the very least, above or below it. You've found a place to rest your head and stow your goods, maybe even cordoned off a little private nook to "get the repopulatin' on." But now you face an entirely new kind of menace, not kept so easily at bay with a shotgun or broken bottle: *tackiness*.

Chin up, pilgrim. You may not be able to singlehandedly rebuild civilization. But there's no reason you can't bring a little to your new digs.

It all begins with looking around at the space that fate has led, or chased, you to. With just a little imagination, resourcefulness, and ingenuity, you can make any post-apocalyptic pad the kind of place that others would kill to live in—well, even more so than they already would.

LET'S TAKE THE DIFFERENT TYPES OF SPACES YOU'RE LIKELY TO HOLE UP IN, ONE BY ONE:

Making the House You've Taken Over Your Own

We have already learned in Chapter 1 how, according to Aftermathe-matics, in the end times people will massively outnumber possessions. Well, the same holds true of habitations. Forget everything you've heard in real estate seminars and read in the financial pages–the coming years are going to be what experts call a "squatter's market." But who says you can't squat in style?

The main consideration here is that, if you were drawn to this still-standing, relatively habitable structure, others will be too. Therefore, you'll want to take advantage of a key principle called **defensive design.** This is, in brief, the art of making your home look like a fortress, without feeling like one.

There are a number of fun, inexpensive ways to keep interlopers at bay by minimizing "Curb Appeal". It starts with a Non-Welcome Mat–we recommend big, neon or other brightly colored lettering on a mat so large it can be seen from the street. Don't bother with those artificial "Beware of the Dog" placards that are in vogue now. In the lean times to come, that will be tantamount to putting up a sign that reads, "Dinner is Served!"

Another way to send the message "That's right, keep limping, punk" to would-be "unplanned visitors" is through the creative use of **no-man's-landscaping.** If any plant life has survived on your new front lawn, use whatever sharp implements are at your disposal to create a tableau of disturbing images. **Some suggestions:**

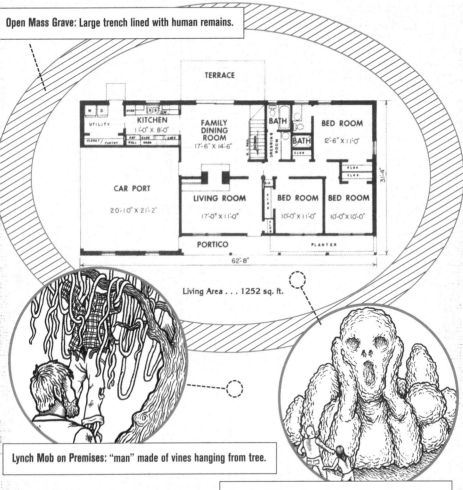

Open Mass Grave: Large trench lined with human remains.

TERRACE

UTILITY
KITCHEN
11'-0" X 8'-0"

FAMILY DINING ROOM
17'-6" X 14'-6"

BATH

BATH

BED ROOM
12'-6" X 11'-0"

CAR PORT
20'-10" X 21'-2"

LIVING ROOM
17'-0" X 11'-0"

BED ROOM
10'-0" X 11'-0"

BED ROOM
10'-0" X 10'-0"

PORTICO

PLANTER

62'-8"

31'-4"

Living Area . . . 1252 sq. ft.

Lynch Mob on Premises: "man" made of vines hanging from tree.

Abandon All Hope: large topiary of Munch's *The Scream*.

Although obviously paint is going to be in short supply, you really ought to consider touching up the exterior. Simple, designer touches like a few artful splashes of "dripping blood red" can go a long way toward repelling the queasy. Conversely, if a nuclear blast has left the poignant silhouette of a family intact on the outside, cover that thing up right away! **The last thing you want to convey is, "A picture-perfect family of four is no longer in residence—come on in!"**

As a final note, the front door should obviously not be left to function as such. If you have an axe to spare, leaving one lodged in there to send the message, "tried to break in but failed." Then, you and your family should only enter from a hidden side or rear door, garage, cellar, or—ideally—a cat door.

bad

INTERIOR

With the inside of the house, your considerations are equal parts aesthetic and pragmatic. Basically, if anyone makes it inside, you'll need to beat a hasty retreat.

There are a number of renovations you'll want to make to turn this into both a livable and survivable space. For example, consider **a closed floor plan.** Sure in latter days, we enjoyed being able to serve our guests in the dining room directly from the kitchen. But think how much more pleasant it will be when you can easily blockade yourself in the kitchen (the place of handy knives and fire). The same goes for any other pesky "half-walls" or breakfronts built into the house. Brick them up, pile them high with non-flammables, close them off. They may have once enhanced a sense of "airiness," but when the air can be filled with toxins or live ammunition at a moment's notice, where's the charm in that?

On a more purely design level, think about the types of adversaries you wish to prevent from feeling "at home" inside your walls. For instance, in the event of the Rapture, you will almost certainly be visited by the minions of Antichrist. This is a great reason to decorate not only with crosses aplenty, but also earth-tone, flowing, natural-material touches—the "hippie sense" that Christ was known for—not the "clean design" emblematic of the Beast.

Fortunately, one currently popular design feature will continue to serve its original purpose and much more in the future: the kitchen island. How delightful that, in most houses built in the past 15 years, you have built-in higher ground to escape to in the event of flood, fire, or rampaging cyber-squirrels. In fact, if anything, this idea wasn't extended far enough. Think about putting in living room, bedroom, and bathroom islands. The roof's the limit!

VOLCANIC RED

RUSTIC DECAY

MUTANT GREEN

from **Bunker** to
Bungalow

What if the outside is still not really accessible, and you're stuck inside a bomb shelter, military-grade bunker, or panic room[29]?

Take heart. You may be hemmed in physically by four walls, but aesthetically, there are no limits to your imagination!

A few touches of ingenuity and an ironclad determination to maximize your livable space are all you need to transform this into a place you'd want to spend not just the next 10 years, but the next 10,000 years.

In particular, we recommend the following modifications:

Defining Your Space

This is particularly key, in light of the fact that you may be sharing this chamber with anyone from neighbors to your entire town to—worst-case scenario—in-laws.

First things first: a clean, bright line painted between yours' and others' territory. Remember how this trick has been used in sitcoms throughout history to separate squabbling roommates? Now you can enjoy the same hearty laughter you used to watching *The Brady Bunch* reruns every time you glance across the line to your co-inhabitants. Make it a game: you're Marcia, and they're Jan. (Or, if you're feeling particularly daring, reverse it.)

The strategic use of accent colors will not only mark your distinctive sense of style, it will mark off your possessions and loved ones. If you have plentiful coloring agents, keep your area's colors fresh and, if possible, wet. A neighbor's bratty kid whose hands are smudged in your colors is all but an admission of territorial incursion. Likewise, keep your turf your own with the use of throw pillows—especially if you fill them with rocks or heavy material that can be thrown for maximum pain.

[29] Or its New York equivalent, a "free-floating-anxiety nook."

MAKING IT YOUR OWN

Cheer things up in this unremittingly artificial environment through the use, wherever possible, of natural materials. Be creative with whatever is at hand, and don't get attached to old preconceptions. If you're looking for something to make a rug out of, remember: the hair and skin of the deceased are every bit as "natural" as seagrass and jute.

Another old idea you'll want to to rethink is that of northern, eastern, southern, and western exposures. Once desirable in a house or apartment, in a world where you're consigned to a bunker, they can be deadly. Instead of looking for places in your new home where you can "bring the outside in" the priority now is more about "keeping the outside out."

Make sure to remove lead paint and asbestos. Remember, while the outer world is toxic, you want your home to be a retreat, a castle, a "non-deadly space" to call your own. Also, if you save these materials up, you'll have handy sources of poison to use against rival tribes/noisy next-door neighbors/owners of houses you covet.

Finally, you'll need to put your ingenuity to the test in order to maximize storage space. If you've got high lead-shielded ceilings, get used to thinking vertically. Be prepared to barter away or incinerate anything that isn't either 1) edible or 2) stackable. If it's not safe to ascend to the surface anyway, don't waste that ladder—turn it into a much more useful (not to mention decadent!) "climb-up closet."

EXTREME MAKEOVER
CAVE EDITION

Depending on what exactly has happened to the world, a cave can provide a usable living space for those who want access to the outside world, without the conspicuous desirability of a man-made structure… and all, of course, on a budget that may literally be comprised of shoestrings.

Understandably, you may be wary about this prospect at first. *Caves are for bats,* you might be thinking, *or those who want to remain unaware of the latest celebrity news.* Well, here's the good news: with the right eye for light, space, and detail, a cave can also be your paradise beneath the Earth's crust.

Here's a few tips on how to use a designer's eye (once it adjusts to the dark) to bring out the subterranean splendor.

COLOR: In short, don't be afraid of it. Of intruders, bears, snakes, guano, yes. But not of color. From his earliest days on/under Earth, man has used paint, chalk, enemy blood, and whatever bright materials were at hand to brighten up those dreary cave interiors. Who says you need a successful mammoth hunt to commemorate before turning your bedroom wall into a work of art?

UPDATE THE LOOK: With a cave, this is ridiculously easy. Pretty much anything you bring in that was created by post-Stone-Age man will accomplish the task.

TASK LIGHTING: In a word, do your tasks anywhere where there is lighting. You'll thank yourself later.

CHOOSE A FOCAL POINT: Build your design concept around one part of the cave you feel will be the centerpiece of family and social activity. It could be anything, really: the fire pit, the water source, a particularly big rock… did we mention the fire pit already?

A TOUCH OF LUXURY: Don't be afraid to bring a healthy dose of your modern comforts to your pre-modern dwelling. Want to organize your stash and have a concave corner to spare? Consider putting in a **California cavern.** Happen upon a natural warm-water spring or, at the very least, moisture-ridden hole? Transform it into a relaxing **soaking tub.** Have access to animal fats and flammable fibers? Put in a series of scented candles, which will serve the double purpose of enhancing the romance and warning you of gas leaks.

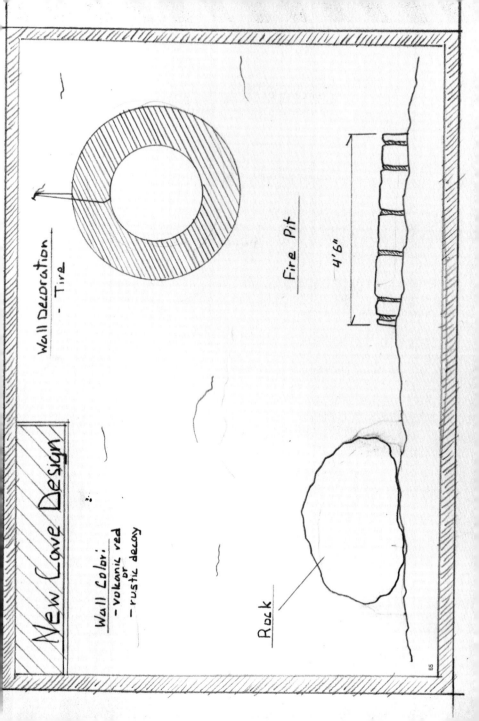

New Cove Design

Wall Color:
- volcanic red
  or
- rustic decoy

Wall Decoration
- Tire

Fire Pit

4'6"

Rock

65

BEFORE WE BLOW

DON'T WAIT—BUILD YOUR DREAM REFUGE NOW

As we have seen, the possibilities available to the aesthetically conscious apocalyptic are limited only by the imagination. But what if you can already envision the place you want to spend your—and humanity's—last days?

You can see it so clearly in your mind: You (and optionally, others) kicking back, sittin' on your own porch, sipping lemonade, and watching the world die.

If you've got the money, there's no time like the present. Even if you think you don't, remember that whatever you do have will soon be worthless. So why not make the most of it now?

Here's a few tips for making your "home away from hell" a reality.

Location: Avoid places of any human significance whatsoever.

SIZE/LAYOUT:

BEDROOMS You want just enough to accommodate you and your loved ones, no more. Avoid the temptation to put in a guest room. Trust me—someone who's fled the final tribulations of the human race and asks to "crash" with you is just going to wear out their welcome.

BATHROOMS In the absence of reliable human infrastructure, we recommend a hybrid septic/bucket/hole-in-ground system. Also, don't skimp on the number. You don't want your daughters too busy fighting each other to help fend off armies of mutants.

KITCHEN Leave ample space for the latest pre-modern appliances. Walk through and ask yourself, "Could I comfortably churn butter/skin and gut a warthog here?"

LAND Say goodbye to "no more than you can maintain" and hello to "as much as you can defend." Plus, remember the flood of cheap migrant labor about to come your way....

FINANCING Prudence is for the pre-apocalypse. With debt collection a near-impossibility in the end times, take on that 45% interest rate loan. Hell, make it an adjustable rate—what's the likelihood the bank will even be standing in seven years? Best of all are timeshares, or, as they will soon be known, "timekeeps."

CHAPTER 3

CLOTHING

DRESS FOR DISTRESS

It's a nightmare you've probably had countless times: you're going about your business when an air-raid siren goes off, a blast shatters the windows, or a loud, unearthly hum fills the air. You and your family, friends, neighbors, and fellow citizens (and oddly, someone you went to high school with but who's, like, *somehow still the same age as they were then*) run for cover, descending to the nearest shelter or holing up in a secure facility, waiting for news of what has just happened and what you should all do now…

…and suddenly, you realize you're *totally naked!*

You wake up in a cold sweat, terrified at the prospect of such catastrophic public embarrassment, though soon relieved to remember that you are still safely in possession of a complete wardrobe.

But, you can't shake the disturbing feelings the dream left you with. You spend the rest of the night tossing and turning, asking yourself over and over, **"What if the world did go up in a massive fireball? What would I have to wear?"**

The answer, my friend?
EVERYTHING

OUR SMOLDERING CIVILIZATION
THE ULTIMATE
SECOND-HAND STORE

Combine every single Friday-after-Thanksgiving, December 26th, January 2nd, Presidents' Day, and 5 a.m. Wal-Mart opening when a hot new video game console or talking furry monster toy is unveiled.

A drop in the bucket, compared to The Day After. Or, as it shall come to be known by future chroniclers of man, The Biggest Shopping Day in Human History.

It doesn't matter if the clothes you're currently wearing get scorched off, seized by sentient apes eager to assert their dominance, or simply prove inadequate to the deep arctic freeze overtaking the Earth. If you're one of those left standing by the Great Event, you're almost certainly going to need something new to drape over yourself.

But when you take a look around your new world, you're going to see something extraordinary: an entire, highly productive consumer society's textile output lying before you, at no cost—an endless rack of actual "steals."

So how do you get there first, and get what you want?

BEAT THE CROWDS!

THIS IS NO LONGER A METAPHOR. WE RECOMMEND THE FOLLOWING METHODS:

BASEBALL BAT

Show no mercy. Most of your fellow would-be "consumervivors" will be blinded by the sudden wealth of "shopportunities"[30] and not have your foresight. The kind of foresight that will lead you to delay your "lootacy"[31] long enough to make a detour to the sporting-goods store first.

BUILDING COLLAPSE

Childishly simple. If your shopping district is located in a still-hot war zone, draw enemy fire to your position. If destruction has already wrecked the area, one push in the right place should do the trick. Once the dust clears, simply roll up your soon-to-be-replaced sleeves, and start digging.

MASS PANIC

Developmentally-disabled-childishly simple. You're talking about a crowd already on its last nerve and predisposed to go bonkers on the slightest pretext. Some of our favorites include:

"Look, a filthy [Member of Hated Ethnic Group]!"[32]

"Oh no! The [Entity That Did This to Us]! They're coming back for more!"

"Hey! This guy right here—he's [Radioactive/Contagious/an Alien in Disguise]!"

"Dear God! Flying wolves—with cobras for tails!"[33]

"Here comes Jesus, and he looks pissed!"

Does all this sound a little cruel and amoral for your tastes? Don't feel bad.
Trust us: these people would do the exact same thing to you if they were in your shoes.
So why shouldn't your shoes be that last pair of Manohlo Blahnik "rubble editions?"

---

[30] If not by a bomb blast or the maniacal Dr. Ophthalmo's fearsome "Blinding Rays"

[31] OK, admittedly, that was pushing it.

[32] Use the strongest epithet you know. There's no more "politically" anything, let alone "correctness." However, be warned that, due to radiation, new ethnic groups might be springing up at any time, some of them with superpowers.

[33] A bit of a desperation move, but right now people will pretty much believe *anything*.

BROKEN WINDOW-SHOPPING 101

So now you've got the whole remains of a display window to yourself—an embarrassment of britches, if you will. But time is fleeting. Within moments, the bargain-thirsty mob will be back, and ready to smash your face in with a freshly denuded "ski bunny" mannequin. You are caught perilously between shopping spree and killing spree.

Lifelong shopaholic? This is your last bender, so binge like there's no tomorrow (which there, in fact, might not be).

Don't like to shop? Fear not. This is the last time you'll have to pull clothing off of something your tribe didn't just kill.

In either case, the mantra running through your head now should be "grab fast, grab smart."

See something you like? Take multiples, in as many colors as they have. Imagine the fun of "mixing it up" with a different tank top for *every month of the year*.

Look for neutral pieces, classics that will last forever—because frankly, they won't have a choice.

Be flexible with sizes. If it won't cut off your circulation, congratulations! It's your size.

Have kids or planning to? Pick up a size too large. Hell, pick up five sizes too large. You never know how many mutated tentacle-like arms will have to fit through those sleeves.

This is going to be hardest to swallow, but in terms of fabrics, go for manmade over natural. Polyester, dacron, rayon, polydacron blend—these are your new watchwords.[34] "100% Cotton" might as well read "100% Lying in Tatters on the Desert Floor."

Abandon the concept of seasonality. Who knows what temperature the Earth will be tomorrow, let alone three months from now? As far as anyone knows, everything is off-season now—and isn't that the best time to buy anyway?

[34] Unless, of course, the apocalypse was caused by a freak textile mishap that resulted in a race of supersentient polyester.

Rapturous Finds

Locating the Best Formerly Christian-Occupied Garments

Okay, first the bad news: You are not one of God's elect. While the true Christians have been "raptured" up to heaven, you are consigned to 1,000 years of Satanic chastisement.

And now for the good news: Christian lore has it that those who are taken will go up just as the Lord made them, in their birthday suits.

So what happens to all those tens of thousands of shirts, skirts, slacks, blouses, hats, shoes, and accessories?

Like the sinful nonbelievers despised by the Sovereign of the Universe, all those "gently used"[35] clothes get "Left Behind."

Just think of it: any clothing item you want, direct to you by Heavenly consignment. But how do you find what you want? Use the map on the following two pages as your guide to the best that the best abandoned.

---

[35] And not just gently–piously.

LEFT BEHIND:
The Armageddon Shopping Guide

Pacific Northwest:
Flannel, Hiking Boots,
Anything made of Gore-tex

West Coast:
Yoga Pants, Inline Skates,
Thongs

Texas:
Cowboy Hats,
Skillet-Sized Belt Buckles,
Cowboy Boots (untouched by dirt)

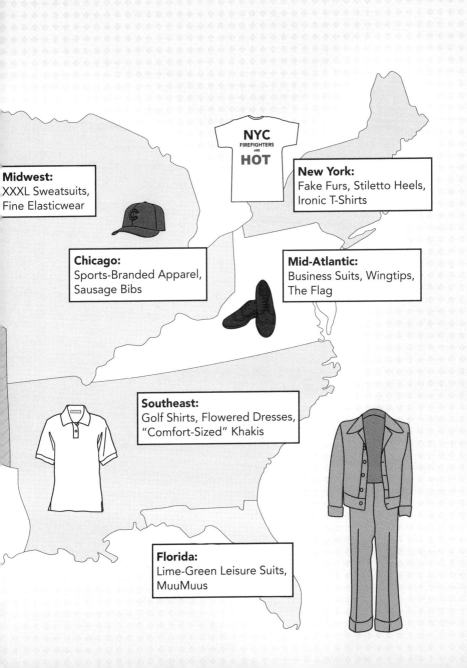

Midwest:
XXXL Sweatsuits,
Fine Elasticwear

NYC
FIREFIGHTERS ARE
HOT

New York:
Fake Furs, Stiletto Heels,
Ironic T-Shirts

Chicago:
Sports-Branded Apparel,
Sausage Bibs

Mid-Atlantic:
Business Suits, Wingtips,
The Flag

Southeast:
Golf Shirts, Flowered Dresses,
"Comfort-Sized" Khakis

Florida:
Lime-Green Leisure Suits,
MuuMuus

PICKING OUT YOUR POSTWAR-DROBE

Millions, if not billions, of human beings have perished, been enslaved, or are rapidly heading toward one of those conditions. Homes, cities, whole nations, and continents have been overturned and uprooted. The history of mankind has effectively been set back thousands of years.

For perhaps the first time in your life, you are forced to come to a difficult realization:

It's not all about you.[36]

But that's no reason to dress like it isn't.

Among the precious few things in your life you have control over now, your look is one of them. Think of the devastating global upheaval you have just lived through as a supercharged Image Consultant, going through your closet, throwing out some items, donating others, tssk-tssking, and murmuring, "Oh honey, *please*," "How did you wear this and not get arrested?" and "Hel-lo! Pre-Armageddon just called: it wants its look back."

In other words, it's not just Planet Earth that's getting a makeover.

But with the baffling multitude of clothing choices available to you now, where do you even begin?

---

[36] Although numerically speaking, it is, in fact, hundreds of thousands of times more about you than it was before.

the Occasion

With the human calendar—and indeed, millennia of accumulated timekeeping conventions—thrown by the wayside, it's more important than ever to mark those "special moments" by your choice of garb.

FORMALWEAR

Never before in human history has the black tie been more optional. But that hardly means the simple elegance of black-on-white is obsolete. Indeed, in a world where it may require decades of experimentation to re-perfect color-dyeing technique, the woman's "little black dress" may be the easiest clothing item to replicate. As for men, forget the tux. Go out and hunt down an actual penguin suit. You can eat the meat, and no more of those annoying cuff links you're always losing!

HOLIDAYS

Now here's something to celebrate: The dictatorial grip of the holiday calendar has finally been broken. Slip on that adorable "blotchy images of trees and ornaments" Christmas sweater any time it's cold (which may well be all the time). No Labor Day? Live out your long-held fantasy of wearing white all year long. And since no one knows when Valentine's Day really is, you ladies can tie yourself into that tiny red leather corset _every single day_!

PARTY ATTIRE

With no deadlines, curfews, or morning trains to catch, you'll probably want to party every night. But for those _truly_ festive times, you'll want something special on hand. Let the occasion dictate the style. For example, what says "We just survived a marauding band's attack" better than a simple, classic, necklace of marauder-ears? The Robot Governor has decided _not_ to puree your mother into machine lubricant? What better occasion to show some flesh of your own in a saucy "nut-and-bolt mini"?

Top Trends For The End

FASHION EXPERTS MAKE THEIR FORECASTS

Dwayne Kajagoogov, a.k.a. "Jagov"
"The future's going to be all about the absence of color. Be bold and mournful with your use of gray. Why settle for a plain-jane 'charcoal' when something more morbid will do? A little 'splash of ash,' judiciously applied, will really bring out the hollows in your cheeks. My prediction: black will be the new—and final—black."

Mimi Jungfrau, *Fifteen Magazine*
"If the world blows up, you should just like blow off whatever your lame parents tell you and totally wear whatever makes you feel fun, young, not, like, tied down to some stupid husband with heart problems and cholesterol issues. When you find a piece of clothing, you should be all 'Is it short, tight, and totally rebellious?' I am *so* there!"

Vampira, Supermodel/Entrepreneur
"Asteroid hit the Earth? Work it, girl. Bad guy wipes out half the planet? Own it. Little green men take over? Put on your face, slip into something smoking, and go get up in their whatever-they-got-for-faces. Your attitude is your latitude, girl. You gotta be all, 'You took away my man, my apartment, and my party pad, but you are *not* touching this look.' Mmm. Damn. Did I mention 'working it'?"

Hobo Joe, *Under the Bridge*
Everyone will look fabulous!

CARE AND MAINTENANCE:
KEEPING YOUR END TIMES LOOK TIMELESS

This time we'll start with the good news: as of the day human civilization as we know it cease to exist, every item of clothing you own or acquire *automatically becomes "retro."*

But even the most fashionably vintage wardrobe—while now immune to the ravages of fashion critics and trend-chasing clothing marketers—is not immune to the ravages of time and use.

How do you ensure that button-down-Oxford-and-surfer-shorts ensemble keeps looking just as perfect, from the day the Machines rise all the way through the brief, tyrannical rule of King TiVo the Selector?

Start with common sense. If you kill and gut a particularly plump-looking Tree Frog, don't get any blood on your clothes. It will take forever to get the stain out in a world where you have to make your own club soda bubble by bubble. And don't leave items out to line-dry within enemy flaming-arrow range. That's just setting yourself up for unsightly "siege burns."

Follow the care and washing instructions on the label to the extent possible, with just a few modifications.

	Where it says "tumble dry," strap it to your belly, curl yourself up on top of a hill, and let 'er (okay, you) roll.
	Where it says "machine"-wash, substitute "concubine." If the sun can still be seen through the Earth's atmosphere, go take advantage of "nature's dry cleaner"—the kind that can actually do the job in an hour, with no worries about lost claim tickets.

Another key to wardrobe longevity is organization.
One suggestion: arrange items by type, then color, then animal-hide, then imperviousness-to-toxic-stinging-insects. And don't throw out that sun-bleached human ribcage—use it to store extra buttons, clasps, and latches for repairs.

All these suggestions will help maintain your items' integrity. But what about preserving a more important quality: their fashionability? Easy. Simply pre-stress them. Don't wait until it's dirty to stone-wash that shirt. Start the rips and tears *you* want in your clothes now, rather than just leaving them to chance/ape attacks. And the seemingly endless months of acid rain? Those are just God's way of saying, "I want you to have badass jeans."

PRE-STRESSED

Nuclear Winter Collection

Toxic

Earrings from the Geiger collection and an antibiotic handbag turn your Hazmat into a "Zazzmat"!

Put on the Shine

From a distance, the Robots think you're one of them. Closer to home, catch a little sunlight and desalinate water on your ass.

Lookin' Phat

Clever, dual-purpose "pelvic pads" plump up your hips to say "come hither" to potential babymakers, but "stay thither" to potential slavemasters.

Glamour

Get the Lead On

Finally! Your world-famous collection of pewter salt-and-pepper-shakers gets a second life as a radiation-proof "hoodie" for your children. The "yummiest" clothing item since edible underwear. (NOTE: Not recommended in canibal/flesh-eating-extraterrestrial-run ones)

Fur-getaboutit

As the glaciers rise and oceans freeze, why bother with those skimpy stoles of yore? Wear the whole mink! Look and feel hot, and if you've got a date, a musk gland is always conveniently "at-hoof."

Man's Best Fit

Why settle for wool when you can have Will? "Flesh out" your wardrobe with this smart, all-weather pullover that tells enemy humans "don't mess with me", and nonhuman overlords, "I will totally sell out my race to serve you." Best of all, it's 100% recycled!

DRESS SMART, SCRAMBLE SMARTER

WHEN THE APOCALYPSE COMES, YOU MAY ONLY HAVE TIME TO LEAVE HOME OR SEEK REFUGE WITH THE CLOTHES ON YOUR BACK. WE THEREFORE RECOMMEND YOU WEAR THE FOLLOWING ITEMS ON YOUR BACK AT ALL TIMES:

3 undershirts (Don't forget the antiperspirant. No one wants to be "pitted out" in perpetuity.)

4-5 overshirts and blouses (preferably breathable fabrics—in case you need to breathe through them until the toxin settles.)

2 heavy winter coats (the more pockets, the better—they are the safe deposit boxes of the future.)

BELOW YOUR BACK, OF COURSE, YOU'LL WANT TO BE WELL-EQUIPPED AS WELL: 7 pairs of underwear (not counting the clean pair you'll want on in case you don't survive the cataclysm but your mother does.)

5 pairs of pants (no button-flies, please, unless you fancy being lasergunned during a pre- or post-excretory "fumbling session".)

8-10 pairs of shoes (a tight fit, sure, but just think how good it will feel as you take each successive pair off.)

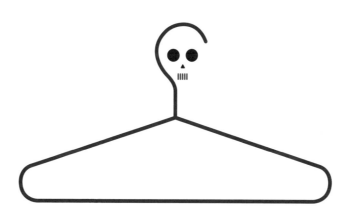

CHAPTER 4
SOCIAL LIFE

How to Win Friends
&
Influence Mutants

Solitude, glorious solitude. How many times have you wished for it while stuck in traffic, jostling for elbow room on a subway train, or crammed into a shipping container with your fellow America-bound refugees?

Well, if the blackened hellscape you're about to inhabit is going to prove anything, it's this: Sometimes wishes do come true.

Which is not to say this won't be a challenge. No longer will just a good man be hard to find—any man will. That's why you've got to make every social encounter—friendly, romantic, familial, co-scavenging—count.

Think of it as one of the countless opportunities this untested new world will offer. It's a chance to start over with brand new expectations. Let's say you were a dysfunctional, unpopular, mildly sociopathic wreck before. Now you can continue to be, but—in the absence of other options—people will simply have to put up with it. After all, considering how much the world has changed, why should you?

Let's meet a few of your new co-terrestrials, shall we? Given the likely numbers, it shouldn't take that long.

FRIENDS, ROAMERS, EX-COUNTRYMEN: WHO ARE THE PEOPLE ON YOUR PATCH OF TURF?

Hiya, Neighbor! Hands off My Stuff.

You've followed the advice in Chapter 2, and located and settled into your new home. Depending on how bad the world-ending cataclysm is, habitable spaces are going to be hard to come by. Meaning, you're not going to be alone for long. Furthermore, others may not be as "cool" with solitude as you are. After all, if misery loves company, post-apocalyptic misery has wild passionate sex with and continues to stalk it, even after it clearly has a new boyfriend.

There are two classic ways to approach your fellow squatters, depending on their temperament, likely willingness to cooperate, evident vulnerability, and of course, visible stash.

1) The Welcome Wagon

A festive weed bouquet, a few strips of cured ferret, maybe a gourd of your famous homemade Mosquito Vodka. It doesn't take much to make newcomers feel "at habitation." Just making the gesture sends the friendly, welcoming message: *There are bears around, but together maybe we can outnumber them.*

2) The Weapons Wagon

A carefully laid trap, a neatly dug pit full of pungee sticks, a quick late-night raid on their camp. Again, nothing too fancy is required. Just a simple, elegant assertion of your territorial dominance—no urination required.

KEEPING UP WITH

the Uggs

1517

1515

Jt's a simple fact. People are never going to be exactly the same, even when there are perhaps only dozens of them left. Each of us evolves, acquires, and makes tiny, feeble attempts to reconstitute a once-advanced civilization at our own pace.

So why drive yourself crazy trying to compare yourself with those ensconced nearby? Maybe your neighbors have concocted a slightly less bitter fertility potion. Maybe they've built a bigger stewpot, or figured out how to stretch the tanned hide of a wild boar over their signal drums with less unsightly wrinkling.

It's useless to fret. All you can do is be the best survivor you can be.

That, or sneak in and steal their superior goods under cover of night.

Tribe, Tribe Again

What if you've decided that cooperation, not confrontation, is the best way forward? But maybe the Others are not convinced? Short of taking them prisoner,[37] you can establish trust and camaraderie through a number of fun, easy community-building activities:

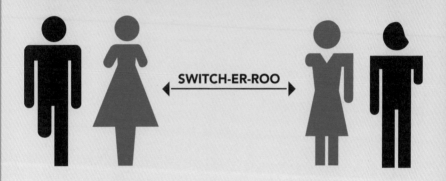

SWITCH-ER-ROO

1) MATE SWAPPING
Just like the famous "key parties" of the 1970s helped bind America together as one, now too there's no social divisions a little "free lust" can't heal.

2) TRUST CIRCLE
Have the members of both groups form one big circle together. Continue to stay this way indefinitely, so no one can try anything untoward without being spotted.

3) BARRICADE RAISING
Who needs a barn like those (now) super-advanced Amish? You've determined you have common enemies—everyone lend a hand to pile up as many rocks and sticks as you can get to stay in place.

4) CIVIC ORGANIZATIONS
There's never not a good time for adults to wear tall hats and intoxicate themselves *en masse*. Form groups based on common heritage (Cold-Landers, Subterraneans), mutual interests (spear-fishing, wound-binding), or—ideally—shared hatred of another ("Let's kill those stupid Subterraneans!")

[37] Not that there's anything wrong with that.

THE POST-NUCLEAR FAMILY

-------------- *Maintaining Hearth and Hovel* --------------

As with so many other aspects of your life, an earth-shattering trauma offers a unique chance to reassess and reinvent. This is certainly true of the family unit, whose traditional structure may change as priorities shift to more "surviving winter" and less "surviving Thanksgiving with boozy Uncle Walt."

Nomadic? No Cry

What if you're not so much of the "stay-in-hole" kind of person?
Like to keep on the move? You may be a candidate for a **roving band**
Use the following guide to pick the one that's right for you.

Hunter-Gatherers

STRENGTH: Efficient, good division of labor

WEAKNESS: Never talk anything but "shop"

Gatherer-Hunters

STRENGTH: Spend much less time on the whole "hunting" thing

WEAKNESS: Significantly lower-protein diet

Borrower-Bargainers

STRENGTH: Can find or acquire everything they need, temporarily

WEAKNESS: Usually on the run from someone

Kvetcher-Worriers

STRENGTH: Have foreseen every single possible obstacle, repeatedly

WEAKNESS: Forced to subsist on Hunter-Gatherer leavings—if they haven't spoiled or aren't too "gristly"

Marriage

Let's say you want to stick with the old, tried-and-true, til-death-do-us-part, in-sickness-and-in-health[39] monogamous type of marriage.

This arrangement may serve you well, providing some much-needed stability in a chaotic world—possibly even more than it did before. For instance, that neighbor's spouse you used to covet? Odds are, either they're out of the picture, or they're your spouse now. Problem solved.

But the two of you may have to adjust your conventional notions of gender roles—who wears the loincloth in the family. For example, in a world where bread is hard to make, let alone win, the wife's gardening may shift from "dirty, annoying hobby" to lifeline. On the other hand, that same "vocation-avocation" switch might also be true of the husband's fishing, even if the indispensable tools of "beer," "the boys," and—for the particularly pathetic— "dynamite" fall by the wayside.

For women, the end times offer the potentially reinvigorating prospect of **fourth-wave feminism.** For those who wish to stay home and raise children, the pressures of career and the judgments of their high-achieving peers will be gone.[40] Also gone are the days of impossibly scheduled, perpetually exhausted "Supermoms." Now you can be a hero to your family by doing as little as protecting them from wolves.

For men, the world becomes a simpler, more straightforward place. Instead of channeling your aggressions into watching other men symbolically battle for territory with a pigskin, you can pretty much go outside and do that for real, right down to the pig. Less certain is how NASCAR will translate to this world, but if enough of the American South survives, a way will be found.[41]

However, to avoid the inevitable conflicts that will arise out of such newly redefined roles, couples who intend their marriage to survive what major metropolises will not are advised to peruse and sign the **Post-Apoc Pre-Nup** found on the following page.

[39] Technically, "in slightly less sickness"
[40] As will, most likely, the peers.
[41] See Ch. 7 "Recreation" for a taste of the entertainments to come.

THE APOCALYPSE HOW POST-APOC PRE-NUP

This Agreement, made and entered into this the ___ day of _____ in the year _____, hereinafter to be referred to as "The Before-Time."

WHEREAS, _____ and _____ are currently married and intend to continue to live together as husband and wife, after the earth-shattering cataclysmic event of _____.

WHEREAS, the parties hereto enter into this Agreement with the desire to define the interest which each of them shall have in the greatly diminished, blackened, irradiated, disease-ridden or otherwise damaged property of the other during and after marriage, or after the death of one of them at the hands of merciless _____.

WHEREAS, in the event of dissolution of the marriage by death, divorce, or nighttime raid by _____, the parties desire for this Agreement and the terms thereof to be enforced in any court of competent jurisdiction, whether administered by humans or _____s.

NOW, THEREFORE, for and in consideration of the premises, the continuance of a post-apocalyptic marriage between the parties, it is hereby mutually agreed by the parties:

1. _____ acknowledges that all of the property to be hoarded by _____ is _____'s separate stash, except he or she may barter any part or all of his or her separate property, at any time and in any manner as he or she may see fit, free from interference or claim of _____.

2. Each party agrees that he or she shall not take any action or institute any proceeding that may cause the stash of the other party, whether consisting of livestock, dried food, medicinal herbs, weapons, religious fetishes, firemaking materials, or pre-apocalyptic usable goods to be stolen, nabbed, bartered away, or otherwise nullified.

3. Should there be a divorce after Year 5 of the New Era, the parties agree to attend binding arbitration to resolve the value of the property they are to divide, and/or to resolve their differences in Thunderdome.

IN WITNESS WHEREOF, the parties have hereunto set their hands and seals on the date first above written.

_____
Survivor of the First Part

_____
Survivor of the Second Part

Children & Childrearing

Will raising children be a challenge in the age of Armageddon? Of course. But as a parent, there are quite a few reasons for encouragement:

- If you view "kids today" as a pack of unruly monsters with no regard for law and tradition, you're not an old fuddy-duddy like *your* parents. You're a sharp-eyed observer!

- No positive role models in their lives? Sure. But hey, no negative ones either.

- *Everyone's* family is "blended" now. To the child who protests, "You're not my real dad!" there's finally a good response: "Duh!"

When society as we know it crumbled to the ground, *so did its expectations of parents*. Forget grade point averages, college acceptances, career and spouse choices. If they make it to adulthood without killing each other and propagate the species, you're Ward and June Cleaver.

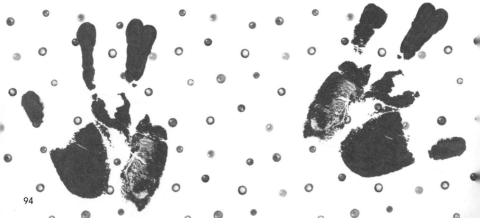

But to keep them in line, you will need to draw upon a few proven post-apocalyptic parenting strategies:[42]

Carrot & Stick

Literally. You can accomplish an amazing amount of discipline by withholding/offering carrots, and penalizing with sticks.

Advanced Carrot & Stick

This new world offers a host of compelling rewards and punishments, many of which are right at hand. "Going to bed without supper" takes on a whole new force when supper is the only meal of the day. Likewise, when their only source of sugar is that which is boiled out of beet mash, a little goes a long way.

Actual Bogeymen

Whether your world is now overrun by fearsome octopus-headed Rigellians, hyper-intelligent-yet-sadistic cloned sheep gone awry, or the very Hounds of Hell,[43] you now have a tangible threat at hand to incentivize your kids to behave, do their chores, or eat their vegetable.

Time Outs

These gain a fresh potency when there is literally *nothing to do.* Five minutes feels like five hours, five hours like ten. And, under the new timekeeping conditions, who's to say it isn't?

[42] Well, they haven't been disproven.

[43] To say nothing of Hell's Sporting Class Dogs and Terriers.

95

ELDERLY RELATIVES: TREASURES OR STRAGGLERS?

They are called many things: "The Greatest Generation" A variety of monosyllables (Nana, Pop-Pop, Goo-Ba-Dee-Goo, etc.). The same thing they were just called a moment ago, only louder.

Whatever you call them, the elderly will have a special place in our après-society. Sure, they won't be able to spoil the grandchildren in quite as conspicuous a fashion come Christmas[44]. And yes, maybe babysitting isn't quite as essential when both parents aren't working, and "Date Night" only consists of Mom and Dad going out for a skate on the giant ice sheet rapidly covering what used to be Arizona.

But these plucky "Senior Survivors" will still have plenty of specialized skills to offer, including:

Volunteering Skills Depending on the extent of catastrophic destruction, human society will likely be left with thousands of abandoned buildings—many of which will become, in essence, museums to our former civilization. And you know what thousands of museums will need: *thousands of docents.*

Part-Time Job Skills Whether as crossing guards, retail store greeters, or airport security screeners, "working retirees" fill in all kinds of small but valuable niches in our society. They are bound to find and fill such roles quickly in the new world, especially when their already-meager Social Security payments dry up entirely.

Survival Skills Today's elderly are scrappy. Many have lived through World War II, the Great Depression, World War I, the Spanish Flu epidemic, the Gilded Age, the Cotton States Exposition, the Panic of 1893, the Trail of Tears, and the Garfield Assassination.[45] "A giant supervillain's tractor beam has stopped the Earth's orbit, dooming it to an endless winter? *Pshaw.* Did I ever tell you about the time the Tsar's army burned down your Gramps's forge?"

Doting Skills Senior citizens put a kindly human face on all our endeavors (along with, in many cases, a doily). Their "soft touch" can help ease relations with our tyrannical nonhuman masters, a surprising number of which might be receptive to a tray of lemon squares.

But the most important function the elderly can play is that of easing the transition back to low-tech society. In a world without driving, computers, or call waiting, their weaknesses will disappear and strengths emerge. They are indispensable sources of valuable pre-industrial lore (though see "Back in My Day…" for assessing that value). And when our tribes need "elders," well, who's already automatically qualified?

44 Or as it will come to be known, "The Nocturnal Flight of Whitebeard."
45 Feel free to put the book down if you "need a minute."

Back in My Day...

Distinguishing Useful Lore from Annoying Nostalgia

Old people have a lot to say. And when our high-speed, attention-deficit-disordered society is blown, melted, or frozen to a halt, we're going to finally have to sit down and listen to it. But how do you separate critical information from the just plain critical? The examples in the following at-a-glance chart should help:

	NOSTALGIA	LORE
Sentimental vs. Practical	"Sundays, the whole family would gather round to listen to the 'Glenn Miller Radio Hour.' I tell you, they just don't make entertainment like that any more…."	"Sundays, the whole family would gather round to listen to Glenn Miller, which was not on one of the lower, sub-5 kilohertz frequencies used by police and civil authorities for emergencies."
Vague vs. Detailed	"Good old Dr. Benson. He'd come over to your house any time of day, give you the once-over, and proclaim you sick or well."	"Good old Dr. Benson. He'd come over any time and check for burns, hair loss, and mouth-bleeding, thereby determining whether radiation poisoning had set in."
Exaggerated vs. Realistic	"Why, I remember when a nickel would buy you a Model-T, and you'd still have change left for a sarsparilla."	"Why, I remember when a hundred dollars'd buy you a Model-T, whose internal combustion engine consisted of a chamber in which a fuel/air mixture was burned, yielding hot gases that exerted pressure on pistons."

"FINAL EMERGENCY" CONTACTS LIST

Forget that yellowed, out-of-date, typewritten list peeling off
your refrigerator. When the Big One comes, you'll want to have
contact information for the following:

___ Relatives (who can be reached by foot or carrier pigeon)
___ Doctor (trained in Western, Eastern, and humors-based medicine)
___ Lawyer (think "largest class-action suit ever")
___ Contractor (someone who can finish the job <u>this</u> <u>epoch</u>)
___ Veterinarian (proficient in animal remedies, recipes)

CREATE A FAMILY EMERGENCY PLAN

Designate a familiar landmark or structures to meet at (ex: "the
smoking ruins of the library," "the hole where our house used to be.")

Ensure emergency supplies are divided equally among the family
("Reginald, you share that iodine with your sister!")

Assign specific instructions to each family member ("You run
screaming through the streets, Dad and I will be captured by storm-
troopers and beg for mercy.")

Determine if friends and neighbors are "Day After" material using the following questionnaire:

I know this person through _____.
a) a mutual friend
b) work, church, or activities
c) meetings at the "Machiavellian Survivalists' Club"
d) a police lineup

I have known this person since _____.
a) college
b) childhood
c) the four years he kept me alive in a Vietcong POW camp
d) the four years he kept me in a Vietcong POW camp

This person has asked to borrow my _____.
a) tools
b) kitchen supplies
c) compass and shovel
d) daughter

I am well-acquainted with this person's _____.
a) family
b) friends
c) array of motion sensors
d) vast library of snuff films

This person would likely sacrifice _____ to save a loved one.
a) his/her life
b) great amounts of money or resources
c) an object of comparable or lesser value
d) to Ba'al

Your ideal post-apocalyptic pal is anyone you answered "c" to.
If you answered "d" to one or more, cross 'em off the list. Don't worry—when the End comes, you'll make new friends!

CHAPTER 5

FITNESS & HEALTH

BE YOUR OWN APOCALYPTICAL TRAINER

"At least you have your health."

In our pre-apocalyptic society, that sentiment has become something of a cliché, a meaningless salve offered to those who have lost a job, seen a relationship end, or watched a freak bolt of lightning set their house on fire, the red-hot cinders from which set the family pet ablaze and running for the car, which then explodes.[46]

After all that and more happens to the entire world, if you survive, your health may indeed be the only thing left in your possession.

What better opportunity, then, to finally give it the attention it deserves?

Along with government, buildings, and millennia of human civilization, the final cataclysm will also blow away something even more firmly entrenched: *your excuses for not living a healthier lifestyle.*

MY EXCUSE NOW	BUT IN THE AFTERWORLD...
Not enough time to exercise.	Nothing but, baby.
Too many temptations around me to stick to a diet.	Ice cream will melt, fudge will run out, potato chips will be the first thing to get crushed.
I drive everywhere.	Even the denizens of what used to be L.A. will be walking.
Too much effort.	Think doing pushups is a chore? Wait 'til you're stonewashing laundry and stalking/killing/skinning breakfast.
Exercise is boring!	Nothing gets the pulse and adrenaline up like fleeing a pack of genetically revived triceratops.

[46] Also a bit of a cliché these days.

THE **DOWNFALL-OF-MAN DIET**

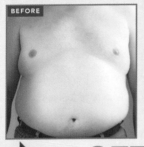

BEFORE

AFTER

GET THIN
AND
STAY THIN!

If you have room among the possessions you grab before fleeing, take your high school prom dress. Because kid, soon you're going to be able to fit in it again![47]

Even after enjoying some of the delicious, inventive recipes in Chapter 1, your newly, inadvertently active lifestyle will burn off the calories faster than you put them on.

Just imagine being able to:

• Eat whatever you want, whenever you want, wherever you can find or steal it—and still keeping (in some cases, barely) your slim physique!

• Look into a mirror—or, more likely, still body of water—and love the skeletal apparition you see.

• Never wear "slimming" stripes, control top stockings, or Spanx ever again—except to keep warm.

A dream? Not at all—well, possibly a heat mirage. But in the post-cataclysmic world, taking the weight off—and keeping it off—can be a snap! How do you do it? By cutting out, posting, and reciting the following five "affirmations":

Apocalyptic Diet Affirmations

• **I do not use food just to make myself feel better—unless what's making me feel bad is gnawing pangs of hunger.**

• **I control the timing and duration of my meals—by means of deadly force if necessary.**

• **I plan out my meals in advance—seconds, even minutes if possible.**

• **I do not snack between meals—unless the snack is going to escape or decompose.**

• **I try and eat something from each of the four food groups: rationed, dried, looted, strangled.**

[47] Actually, a prom dress is a sensible choice for both men and women, as its flame-retardant material may prove lifesaving in the fiery Outlands.

THE ULTIMATE WORKOUT

Every day it seems like fitness experts are trying to cajole us into increasing our workout time. First it was a half-hour weekly, then 45 minutes three times a week, then an hour a day, every day. Come on, guys! Some of us have jobs to go to, or TV programs too valuable to watch closed-captioned on a treadmill.

But their days of yelling at you to "feel the burn" will end when they literally do so. Those 30-45-60-minute workouts they made millions of dollars trying to sell to you will pale in comparison to your *unbelievable new regimen!*

The All-Day Exercise Plan

Take a look at some of the bicep-curling, pec-whaling, bun-steeling drills you'll be running every day.

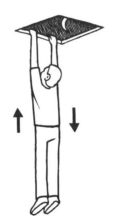

1. Hydro-Lifts

MUSCLES WORKED:
Neck, Quadriceps

REPEAT UNTIL:
Brood quieted, three-tiny-tomato plot watered.

2. Zombie-Checks

MUSCLES WORKED:
Biceps

REPEAT UNTIL:
Daybreak

3. Iron-Digs

MUSCLES WORKED:
Triceps

REPEAT UNTIL:
3X-9's insatiable hunger is filled.

4. Ice-ercise

MUSCLES WORKED:
Full Body

REPEAT UNTIL:
Nuclear Winter turns to Nuclear Spring.
(Bonus: No cool-down needed!)

5. Sunstorm Slalom

MUSCLES WORKED:
Quads, Abs, Hamstrings

REPEAT UNTIL:
The Mighty Ra lessens His rage.

6. Quarantine Sprints

MUSCLES WORKED:
All Leg Groups, Cardio

REPEAT UNTIL:
Your immune system evolves.

7. Tool Holds

MUSCLES WORKED:
Pecs, Biceps, Triceps

REPEAT UNTIL:
The foul Doomio agrees to turn his Doom
Magnet off.

SOYLENT LEAN: STAYING UNFIT FOR ALIEN CONSUMPTION

Although most apocalyptic scenarios will see the human food supply diminish and workload increase, there is one situation in which the opposite may occur: aliens capturing and raising us for their food.

Sure, it *sounds* sweet. You're kept in warm, safe, sanitary conditions, probably naked, fed all you want, and most likely "forced" to mate with another co-speciesist regularly. But remember: that idyllic existence ends the day your cagekeepers deem you USDA[48] Grade-A Dude.

So what can you do to keep your belly from becoming suitable for an extraterrestrial's?

Satisfy the Urge to Purge

Any alien worth its slime has researched enough contemporary human culture to know about our eating disorders. Simply claim you can barely keep anything down—especially with, like, all those *eyes* (possibly on the same creature) watching you.

Crunch Your Abs Before They Do

Remember all those infomercials hawking "flab-smashers" and "exer-gizmos" made of "space-age materials"? Well, guess what materials you're surrounded with now? Anything bolted down (pretty much all they'll leave in your cell with you) is now your personal sit-up machine.

Staple Your Way to Safety

Stomach-stapling has transformed millions of lives, and it just might save yours! You will have to somehow convince your alien masters to procure you a stapler.[49] Then, using whatever lubricants are at hand (the less said here, the better) reach down your own throat and staple around until there's no room for any food to get through. The only danger[50]: an alien watching you swallow your own arm may get jealous.

---

[48] Universal Standard Delicious to Aliens
[49] You might, say, offer to do a little light office work for them.
[50] besides internal hemorrhaging

Jogging for (Your) Life

No matter what happens to the Earth, the likelihood is that someone's going to be on your butt at some point. So there's never been a better opportunity to whip that butt into the taut, firm specimen you used to envy at the beach.

Depending on who engineers our doom or rises to cruel, tyrannical power in the aftermath, you will want to build up the appropriate skills to outpace your pursuer. Use the following guidelines to work on your regimen:

Four Horsemen of the Apocalypse

It's likely that God—what with His Middle East connections—is going to get four primo Arabian thoroughbreds, which have been clocked as galloping up to 30 miles per hour. The world's fastest marathon runners can maintain a 4-minute mile, or about 15 MPH. So this is pretty basic math here: master the training techniques of marathon runners—and then double them.

Race of the Machines

No matter how swiftly they overpower our feeble control systems, our new mechanical masters will not necessarily be the fastest on foot. Where they make up for this, though, is in *stamina*—specifically, not having any limit to theirs. To stay out of metallic harm's way, you must become fleet of foot through robot-unfriendly terrain: rocks, mud, quick-sand, water, and—ideally—the ungraspable depths of love.

Roving Leather Biker Punks

Their entire narrow, cruel, for-some-reason-Australian-accented existence is singularly fixated on the acquisition of gasoline. So you don't have to outrun them—just wander far enough away from paved roads that you become not worth the gas expenditure.

Simian Speed-Trial

Whether it's gorillas, chimpanzees, orangutans, or gibbons, any of our evolutionary ancestors that suddenly become our overlords will have numerous pursuer advantages: humanlike speed, agility with trees and vines, an extra set of thumbs (indispensable if the pursuit is by taxi), and of course, advanced fecal-projectile skills. But we do have one advantage: no fur. The race is yours as long as you keep to hot, arid terrain. This means preserving your internal water supply for as long as possible. When you run, tailor your arm-swing to collect forehead sweat and return to your mouth. Practice long, fast runs while "holding it in"—without devolving into the awkward, slowing "have-to-pee dance." Also, make sure not to run past waterfalls. That's just asking for trouble.

Cybernetically Enhanced Waterproof Killer Bees

Don't bother running. Your only defenses here are a cyber-epinephrine shot and, if you're lucky enough to find some, robo-flowers.

PRESCRIPTIONS FOR DISASTER

There's a lot more to crossing the finish line of the human race than just staying in shape (ie: long, thin, and bony) and eating right (ie: eating). You've got to be prepared for any number of ailments that could befall you. And yes, the finite and ever-dwindling supply of pre-Catastrophe medications is a bit of a drag. But that's just looking at the pill bottle as "half-unrefilled." **Consider never again having to deal with:**

SIDE EFFECTS—Imagine the confidence of knowing you'll always have a moist mouth and a dry anus.

HARMFUL INTERACTIONS—Tired of the seesaw of your antidepressant diminishing erectile function, requiring an erectile enhancer which in turn causes indigestion? In this brave new post-pharmaceutical world, you can safely count on a perpetual state of sad, floppy gassiness.

LONG DRUGSTORE LINES—Because seriously, how long can you dawdle, feigning interest in the delights of the shampoo aisle?

STINGY HMOS—Your medical lifeline shouldn't be in the hands of some faceless insurance-company bureaucrat, but in those of Grambinka, the blind witch.

Even better, why not take your health into your own hands? In the pre-apocalyptic world, "self-medication" may be considered a bad thing. But after the Big One, it's a sign of independence.[51]

   And it couldn't be easier. In the absence of thousands of years of medical advances (just over a hundred, really, unless you consider "mercury drops and ether" advanced), who's to say what works and what doesn't?

   Dr. You, that's who!

   Depending on where your new home is, or what's left of your old one, try out a few of these homebrewed solutions to life's aches and pains.

[51] Not to mention frugality. Grambinka will—no irony intended—rob you blind.

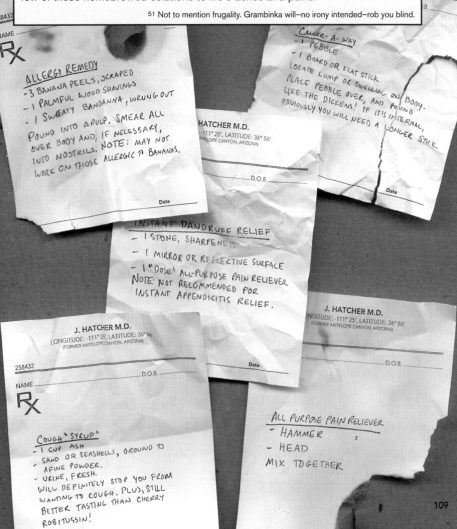

NAME
R̶X̶

ALLERGY REMEDY
- 3 BANANA PEELS, SCRAPED
- 1 PALMFUL WOOD SHAVINGS
- 1 SWEATY BANDANNA, WRUNG OUT
POUND INTO A PULP. SMEAR ALL OVER BODY AND, IF NECESSARY, INTO NOSTRILS. NOTE: MAY NOT WORK ON THOSE ALLERGIC TO BANANAS.

Date

CANCER-A-WAY
- 1 PEBBLE
- 1 BOARD OR FLAT STICK
LOCATE LUMP OR SWELLING ON BODY.
PLACE PEBBLE OVER, AND POUND LIKE THE DICKENS! IF IT'S INTERNAL, OBVIOUSLY YOU WILL NEED A LONGER STICK.

Date

J. HATCHER M.D.
-111° 25', LATITUDE: 36° 56'
ANTELOPE CANYON, ARIZONA)

D.O.B.

Date

INSTANT DANDRUFF RELIEF
- 1 STONE, SHARPENED
- 1 MIRROR OR REFLECTIVE SURFACE
- 1 "DOSE" ALL-PURPOSE PAIN RELIEVER
NOTE: NOT RECOMMENDED FOR INSTANT APPENDICITIS RELIEF.

J. HATCHER M.D.
LONGITUDE: -111° 25', LATITUDE: 36° 56'
(FORMER ANTELOPE CANYON, ARIZONA)

258432
NAME
R̶X̶
D.O.B.

COUGH "SYRUP"
- 1 CUP ASH
- SAND OR SEASHELLS, GROUND TO A FINE POWDER.
- URINE, FRESH.
WILL DEFINITELY STOP YOU FROM WANTING TO COUGH. PLUS, STILL BETTER TASTING THAN CHERRY ROBITUSSIN!

J. HATCHER M.D.
LONGITUDE: -111° 25', LATITUDE: 36° 56'
(FORMER ANTELOPE CANYON, ARIZONA)

Date

D.O.B.

ALL PURPOSE PAIN RELIEVER
- HAMMER
- HEAD
MIX TOGETHER

109

Apocalyptic Ailments, Demystified ---------------

One exciting aspect of the afterworld-to-come is that the bewildering world of health and medicine becomes exquisitely simplified. Sure, there will be those with advanced degrees in medicine and biology struggling to preserve and practice humanity's extensive and hard-won base of medical knowledge.

And it will be adorable.

Jerry

HEADACHES

Cause: Incessant roar of the Flesh Processors

Prognosis: 10 seconds of relief every six hours during shift changes

HEART PALPITATIONS

Cause: Strain of moving around 1000-degree desert-ified Earth

Prognosis: With any luck, a supervolcano's ash will block out the sun.

INDIGESTION

Cause: "Splinter pudding again?"

Prognosis: Maybe you'll get lucky and swallow a termite.

JOINT PAIN

Cause: Overly literal androids' attempts to harvest "elbow grease"

Prognosis: Don't worry—soon they'll be on to the funny bone.

URINARY DISCOMFORT

Cause: Sloppy work of Satan's anti-Semitic "decircumcisers"

Prognosis: If there are any doctors left, you can be sure whose side they're on here.

But on the whole, the dramatically changed conditions of life on Earth will make it refreshingly easier to pinpoint and prognosticate the main causes of human discomfort.

To illustrate, we delve into the bodies of two hypothetical apocalypse-survivors…let's call them "Jerry Lastman" and "Gloria I. Willsurvive.[52]"

[52] Pronounced "WEEL-survEEV." It's French.

Gloria

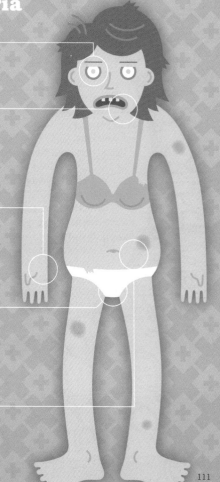

BLINDNESS

Cause: Directly gazing at "The Big One"
Prognosis: How are you with Braille?

TOOTHACHES

Cause: Chattering from Ice Age wrought by renegade asteroid
Prognosis: 40,000-100,000 years to go— but who's counting?

DRY SKIN

Cause: Deployment of Dr. Beelzebubbo's "Earth Dehumidifier"
Prognosis: Eventual intervention of secret agent, or motor burnout

HEMORRHOIDS

Cause: Slave-branding by Mefizo the Tyrannical
Prognosis: Mefizo planning to switch over to "prox card" system soon

INFERTILITY

Cause: Exposure to radiation
Prognosis: Dim. However, children now available for purchase!

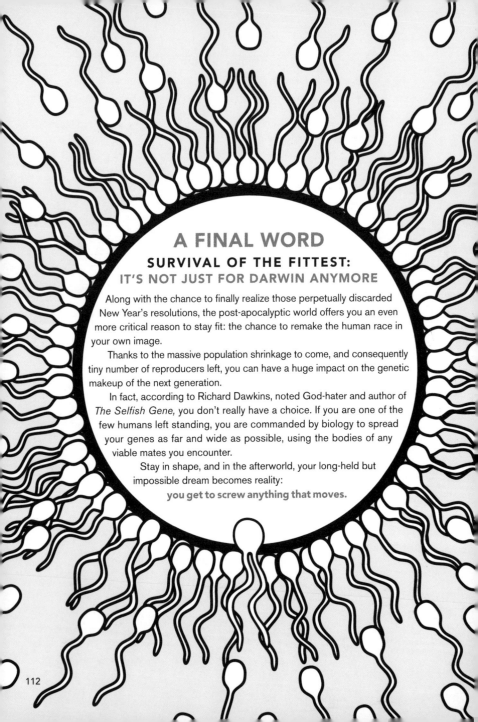

A FINAL WORD

SURVIVAL OF THE FITTEST:
IT'S NOT JUST FOR DARWIN ANYMORE

Along with the chance to finally realize those perpetually discarded New Year's resolutions, the post-apocalyptic world offers you an even more critical reason to stay fit: the chance to remake the human race in your own image.

Thanks to the massive population shrinkage to come, and consequently tiny number of reproducers left, you can have a huge impact on the genetic makeup of the next generation.

In fact, according to Richard Dawkins, noted God-hater and author of *The Selfish Gene,* you don't really have a choice. If you are one of the few humans left standing, you are commanded by biology to spread your genes as far and wide as possible, using the bodies of any viable mates you encounter.

Stay in shape, and in the afterworld, your long-held but impossible dream becomes reality:

you get to screw anything that moves.

EYES ON THE PRIZE!

BEFORE WE BLOW

NO QUESTION ABOUT IT, THERE'S NO BETTER WAY TO GET IN GREAT SHAPE THAN ARMAGEDDON. BUT TO OPTIMIZE YOUR HEALTH REGIMEN, WE RECOMMEND A FEW PRELIMINARY ACTIVITIES TO BEGIN NOW.

EXERCISE
Start walking. Not aerobically, or on a daily basis, just plain start walking away from human habitation. Now.

Add a little more weight to your load, whether in the form of a book, a small dumbbell, or a particularly fat pet. Ask yourself: Am I optimizing my ability to serve my nonhuman masters?

Stretch every day. We recommend postures that may need to be held for long periods: the crouch, the shelter-door-barring push, the fetal ball of fear.

Practice getting into "species-increasing" positions. A complete guide can be purchased for a nickel at participating truck stop restrooms.

HEALTH & MEDICINE
Stock up on those refills now! If you're a hypochondriac, find the one pharmacist in town who hasn't already heard you plead, "it's an emergency" dozens of times.

Make friends with local witch doctors, shamans, and televangelists.

Get a full physical checkup. Make sure and ask plenty of concrete questions, like "which parts could I live without?"

Check with your health insurance plan to see if it covers "out of civilization" providers.

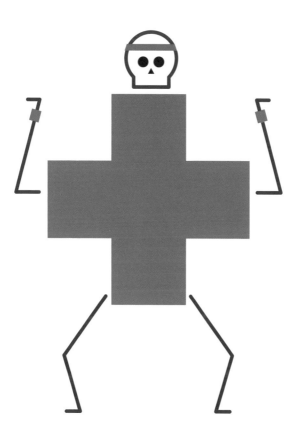

CHAPTER 6

RECREATION, PART 1:

SEX, DRUGS, & ROCKS

"LIVE FAST, DIE YOUNG,
AND LEAVE A GOOD-LOOKING CORPSE."

In the Afterworld, you're almost certain to get 2/3 of that. Hard-living isn't just for burnouts, TV agents, and hotel heiresses anymore. It's a way of life for everyone.

And like any party, it begins and ends with the girl or guy you bring.

LOVE AND DATING
What if You *Are* the Last Man on Earth?

For singles (veteran or new), the end of said world will overturn all the old, tired language of the romantic quest. For instance:

- The "field" you used to play is now likely a blackened desert;
- There are in fact probably very few fish in the sea; and
- It's no longer about finding "Mr. Right" so much as "Mr. Upright."

Reconsider what you used to describe as dating "horror stories." Did any of them actually involve zombies?

Did you ever resent feeling like the only single in a world full of the happily coupled-off? Well, rejoice: you've just entered a world that's *chock full of singles*. And with so few who are actually eligible—or viable—the pressure's off. **You don't need to find your soulmate—just your sole mate.**

So how do you go about finding that (relatively, if not numerically) special someone?

DON'T BE AFRAID TO BE "FAST"

Forget the prior sexual connotations of the term. These days, if you spot a real "catch," you may actually have to catch them—on foot, horseback, or—depending on how much precious fuel you've hoarded—spike-armed motorcycle.

SPEED-MATING

It couldn't be simpler: two lines of people form, exchange basic introductory information ("I can lift a boulder with one arm", "I have a box of matches"), then move down the line to a new partner. If a connection is made, genitally, in nine months at least one of you will know.

CRAG'S LIST

In any habitable area where there are at least three people not of the same clan, a central community board/rock surface is a great place to advertise what exactly you're looking for in a mate: protection, supply-consolidation, a bartering chip, repopulating, or that old romantic standby: hypothermia prevention.

BLIND DATES

"Richard, this is Colleen. Colleen, Richard. You're both…alive." So begins the matchup by a well-intentioned friend of you and a potential candidate. These have a much higher chance of succeeding than they used to, especially if both of you have, in fact, been blinded.

FIND A WINGMAN

Want to set out on your own? Make sure you bring along someone to pump you up, position you for the introductions, and console you for the failures. On the down side, it's best not to have someone do this if they're a romantic rival—which will pretty much describe everyone. On the up side, you may be able to find someone with actual wings.

Common Romantic Pitfalls

Some Armaged-don't's

Walk of Shame Depending on how humanity is clustered, the return from your assignation may be a five-day journey, or three steps across the cave. Whatever the case, don't be too obvious about your recent business. Instead, bring a freshly killed rodent to your tryst, so you can return with it slung over your shoulders, evidence of your "success on the hunt."

Deprivation Goggles "Everyone looks good after a few beers," went the old saying. So you can imagine how delectable they'll look after a few non-dinners. In a time when misguided and poorly remembered hookups may be humanity's best hope for survival, this is a good thing. The only danger: if you're truly deprived, don't get your delectables mixed up. Surely if a praying mantis can remember what order to mate and eat its mate in, so can you.

Actual Pitfalls There's nothing wrong with being a gentleman or a tough woman to impress your date. Just don't underestimate how many things out there can leave actual, painful, and often much longer-lasting impressions on them. Let's put it this way: it's not much use to chivalrously toss your shoulder-fur on the ground in front of your date if you're tossing it onto an acid-puddle teeming with Piranha-bots.

ASK END-TIME EDNA

ADVICE FOR THE FUTURE LOVELORN

Q. I've been seeing this guy I met in my cave for at least three moons now. We're getting along just fine, and our genitals certainly fit, but every time we try to repopulate, one of his kids seems to hop in and ruin the mood by thrashing his tail all over the place. I want to say something, but I don't want to come across as the "evil stepmate." Help!

A. Uh, hel-lo? "Hops?" "Tail?" This guy's a one-man (and probably one-nut) mutant factory. Get out of this relationship, and save yourself for someone with non-fractured DNA. You deserve better, girl!

Q. Every time my partner and I try to make love, we end up choking on volcanic ash and asteroid dust. What do we do?

A. Clearly you need to fill your mouths with something else. Failing that, your classic ball-gag was made precisely for situations like this.

Q. I'm a fit woman with minimal sores and none of my lady parts were microwaved by the Blast. Whenever I go on a grub-forage with a man, I tell him that, and try to wear something that shows off my childbearing hips. Yet they never send a messenger-slave to me the next day. What do guys want these days?

A. Like it or not, sometimes they're just turned off by a woman who knows what she wants—in this case, the continuation of the human race. Don't be in such a rush to advertise your womb. Just because you're filled with existential despair doesn't mean you have to come across as "desperate."

Q. My partner and I are finding it hard to "get in the mood" under these new conditions. What should we do?

A. Imagination and a sense of fun are the key here. Make your surroundings part of the game. Is the Earth one large desert? Have one of you play "scorpion," the other "wounded locust." Being monitored in a cage by tyrannical apes? Pretend you're in a porno movie, and your keeper is an extremely hairy frat boy.

Q. I'm a man who finds it difficult—when I think of those catastrophic days, the devastation, and the screams of millions—to maintain an erection.

A. Obviously it's difficult, but try your best. You need to learn to push that imagery out of your mind, so you can save it for when you're trying to delay orgasm.

Q. I think I've found the woman I want to spend the rest of my life/the harvest season with. She's docile, mashes up a mean "dinner-root," and doesn't balk when I want to go pillaging with the gang. The only problem is, due to her exposure to the Great Sickness, she has a tendency to bleed from one or more orifices. Is this something we need to discuss if we're going to repopulate?

A. As long as she's not bleeding from one particular orifice more than once a moon, you should be good to go. Eyes on the prize, buckaroo!

Settling Down

Just Because the Ground Can't Why Shouldn't You?

You've found that perfect someone, and so far have fended off all attempts to steal him/her in the dead of night. However long the rest of your life is, you've decided you want to spend it with this person. A few steps are in order:

Popping the Question

In some ways, an easier ritual than ever. Here are some sample proposal lines:

*"Will you make me the happiest man/woman on earth?
Or at least not the coldest tonight?"*

*"Baby, I don't want to be with anyone else—
whether or not that becomes statistically impossible."*

"I got two goats and a half-blind cow. Whaddayasay?"

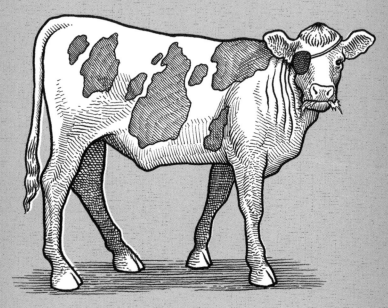

Choosing a Date and Place

Unlike in pre-pocalyptic times, there are no longer huge waiting lists to get into the choicest venues. As a matter of fact, there will soon be more choice locations than ever (Our recommendations: The Uninfected Hilton, the Five-Mile-Underground Inn, and Sandals Coast-of-What-Used-to-be-Called-"Nevada".) But even so, *don't put it off*. The era of year-plus engagements is over. A year from now, who knows how social configurations will have changed? Or whether one of you can be more valuably traded away. Or when exactly it is a year from now.

Registry

Yes, we know, this is always the crassest aspect of the wedding festivities. But you really don't want to find yourself at the reception, unwrapping two palm fronds and feigning happiness as you say, "Oh wow, you made this… out of rocks and mucus?" Besides, after the apocalypse, registration is a snap. Brides—you can just walk around, loudly announcing your preferences. Grooms—depending on the law-and-order situation, you can likely still wander around pointing at desired gifts with a gun. And if the two of you are in an urban(esque) area, simply stride over to your local Crate & Barrel and let them know which one of those two you'd like.

Bachelor Party

The groom's final chance to let down his hair (easier to comb out lice) and go crazy before settling into "respectable proto-society." If you're one of the planners, don't just settle for that old, tired "stripper-jumping-out-of-a-cake" routine. Be creative and use your environment to more surprising effect. Have a stripper jump out of a mysterious green cloud, an army of the undead, or the still-cooling body of the groom's last remaining romantic rival. Lap dances are still okay, but don't forget to bring a wad of winter wheat for tips.

Bridal Shower

It's "Girls' Night Out—Without Being Captured and Enslaved by a Horde of Escaped Cons!" In the past, women were expected to "girl it up" for these things, but nowadays, think simple: no need for a flowery dress when a morning's haul of "borrowed" flowers will suffice. Consider livening this event up with games like:

Spice of Life The classic bridal shower game, where the ladies pass around unlabelled jars of spices and try to identify them by smell. Apres-Apocalypse, you'll simply use the palms of your hands. And in all likelihood, it's all salt. In other words… everybody wins!

What The Bride Says Someone writes down the words that come out of the bride's mouth every time she opens a present. At the end, all the words are read together as "what she'll say on her wedding night." These days, however, this takes on an extra level of fun, since on her wedding night, the bride may need to keep silent until Droid Patrol has swept the area.

Finish the Proverb

As the hostess, you read half of a proverb about love and see who can complete it—with just a few slight updates.

A. "Love means never having to say you're _____."

B. "Better to have loved and lost than _____."

C. "All's fair in _____ and _____.

....

Answers: a. sterile b. to have gone out foraging but returned loveless c. love, whatever's left after war

The Big Day

(well, the other one, anyway)

So now it's finally here: the day you never thought you'd see—especially when the first Mothership began dropping fire from the sky.

You look around and all you see are the loving faces of family, friends, neighbors, slaves, eunuchs, gimps, and abominations.

How do you ensure this will be the most special day of your life?

Don't Sweat the Small Stuff

The caterer didn't boil enough shoe leather. The flower girl was sold and married off to the son of a rival chieftain. It's starting to look like hot molten rain. Don't look at these as setbacks, but rather quirks that will one day amuse with the retelling, and one day long after that, become pivotal details of a myth that allegorically determines whether a condemned man must be executed by strangling or stoning.

Attend to Your Guests

Everyone attending your nuptials has played a key role in your life, or else—due to rationing—they wouldn't have been invited. At some point during the festivities, take a moment to share with them a smile, a kind word, perhaps a small canister of fuel. But don't overdo it. Some have come from a long way away to attend—no need to encourage them to "resettle."

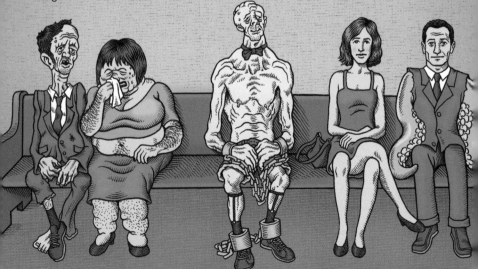

Vows

Some couples like to write their own, some to cobble together what can be recalled from religious texts, others—from once-popular songs, movies, and video games.[53] Here's a few old standards, made new:

For greater stashes, and lesser

For better-fed and for worse

In sickness and in... anyway, moving on...

In ice storms, mud squalls, acid hurricanes, fire-namis, and unappeasable volcanoes

Even when (pointing to ominous interlopers on the horizon) they get here.

Honeymoon

Now the two of you have tied the knot (if under the auspices of your Slave Master, possibly literally). And all you want to do is get away from it all, hide out from the world for just a little while, and never see the light of the day.

Great news: The post-apocalyptic world is *teeming* with such places. With just a little imagination (and tips from Chapter 2), you can turn a humdrum bomb shelter into a "love pit," a hollowed-out pile of rubble into "love among the ruins" or—if it's still got hay around—an abandoned farmhouse into a quaint little "bed-that-ultimately-becomes-breakfast."

---

[53] The origin of the classic vow, "In this life, and the next two."

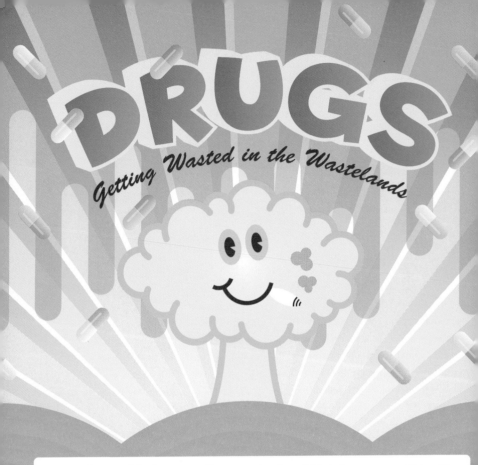

DRUGS

Getting Wasted in the Wastelands

An altered sense of time's passage. Strange and curious sights before your eyes. The melting away of all responsibilities . . .

If you've survived Armageddon, you're getting all that for free anyway. But let's say you're the type of person who wants more of it. You're in luck: Nature's Pharmacy is open for business.[54] What's on offer today, and every day from here on out?

Anything.

That's right. Other than minerals, metals, and inorganic solids, pretty much *anything* found in nature (and quite a few things not) can be crushed, pulverized, and smoked—or mixed with water and sugar and fermented. We can't vouch for the safety of this wide-open pharmacopeia, but then again, you're not exactly after this because you're a health nut, now, are you.

---

[54] Though we should warn you: Nature will still smirk at you if you try to hide your condom purchase by throwing in a pack of gum.

NATURAL HIGHS

No, this isn't the cheesy, after-school special notion of getting high on "life" or "making a difference" or "Christ." We're talking about the human body's seemingly limitless capacity for sending itself into altered states of consciousness. Here are but a few tried-and-true methods:

Breath-Holding

Do it over water or a reflective surface and dig the pretty colors on your face.

Upside-Down-Hanging

You'll start out seeing the world a different way, then just wait until "the red stuff" hits your brain. How else do you think bats manage to cope with all the stress of working the night shift?

Bloodletting

It may not have cured any of the millions who did it medicinally during the Middle Ages, but man, did it make their short, miserable lives that much more "trippy."

Starvation

Certain to be the most popular drug of choice. But be warned: may lead to a severe case of the munchies.

Music
EVERYTHING UNPLUGGED

Like music? Then you'll love the afterworld.
Here's just a few reasons why:

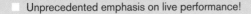

- Unprecedented emphasis on live performance!

- No more "same old tired album collection" to wearily thumb through.

- Pressure to keep current with the latest bands and trends? Gone!

- No more disappointing "sophomore efforts" from bands with killer debut album.

- Dramatic new venues for "arena shows."

- No radio stations, media conglomerates, corporate record labels, or corrupt A&R guys to choose what we listen to—let the (surviving) public decide!

- Much, much easier to see "Monsters of Rock" (not the heavy metal bands, actual creatures sprung to life out of stone.)

If you're a musician, you've just gotten the rare chance to jump right into a band, audition-free. If you were already in a band, now you get a fresh set of cohorts, without even having to call the dreaded "band meeting." And best of all, in a world drastically devoid of entertainment, you will be in great demand—being invited to play everything from weddings (tribe-consolidating, hasty, mass), to forcible baptisms (brush up on that Christian rock!), to public executions (always knew death metal would have its comeback?) to just keeping the hungry mobs from getting restless.

What kind of songlist should you go off of? Fortunately for you, there's already a large and varied repertoire of tunes that, with just a little tweaking, will perfectly resonate with an apocalyptic audience.

Top 25

THIS WEEK	2 WKS AGO	WKS ON CHART	TITLE ★★ No. 1 ★★
1	2	23	INCREASINGLY WILD WORLD
2	1	19	WHEN A MAN CLAIMS A WOMAN
3	3	15	THE ROOF IS LITERALLY ON FIRE
4	4	17	WHAT A CINDERFUL WORLD
5	9	111	WE GOTTA GET OUT OF THIS PLACE… OK, NOW THIS ONE
6	6	27	BABY GOT HUNCHBACK
7	10	39	BRICK HUT
8	8	138	GIRLS JUST WANNA HAVE FOOD
9	7	13	YELLOW SUBTERRANEAN
10	5	9	MR. ROBOTO, SIR
11	13	22	RIKKI DON'T LOSE THAT LUMBER
12	12	15	SMOKE STAYS IN YOUR EYES
13	11	55	ITSY BITSY TEENIE WEENIE YELLOW POLKA DOTS ON JEANNEY
14	15	11	EVERYBODY WANTS TO RULE THE CAVE
15	14	27	ICED, ICED, PRAIRIE
16	20	13	I'D DO ANYTHING FOR LUNCH (INCLUDING THAT)
17	16	44	ALL YOU NEED IS FUEL
18	19	8	HOT OUT HERE
19	17	19	FIGHT FOR YOUR RIGHT (TO SCAVENGE)
20	18	83	THE SOUND OF SILENCE, INTERSPERSED WITH GUNFIRE
21	21	21	HOT ROCKS KEEP FALLIN' ON MY HEAD
22	28	7	PAPA'S UNDER A ROLLING STONE
23	26	11	KILLING ME SOFTLY WITH HIS STICK
24	30	41	DON'T GO TAKING MY STASH
25	22	36	EVE OF DESTRUCTION

LOVE

Just because you're going to spend your afterdays and nights hooking up like a masochistic bait worm is no reason not to plan your conquests well in advance of the End. It will give your fumbling, anonymous trysts that much more of a "thoughtful quality."

Specifically, run through that old mental game "Marry, screw, or kill" (as in, "Which would I rather do to/with/atop this person?") with everyone of the gender(s) you prefer, but simply expand the list to also include soon-to-be-more relevant categories: kidnap, buy, worship, barter away, use-as-human-sandbag-during-flood.

DRUGS

Ordinarily, our advice to the afficionado would be to hoard as much of your most prized substance as possible. In effect: don't smoke 'em if you got 'em. However, if you're the type who cherishes such substances so much that you would prioritize them over items of more immediate need, forget it—there's no way in hell you're staying out of that stash, if only to drown out the deafening roar of the Horsemen's hooves. So, we're in a bit of a paradox here. But then again, what if it's even deeper than a paradox? What if we're all like, one big knock-knock joke in the mind of a six-year-old boy...man...

MUSIC

Even though musical options will be ample and varied, you don't want to find yourself deprived, musically or otherwise. To that end, make up a "Desert Planet" list of your absolutely essential CDs. These will prove indispensable in the future world as hurlable hunting weapons.

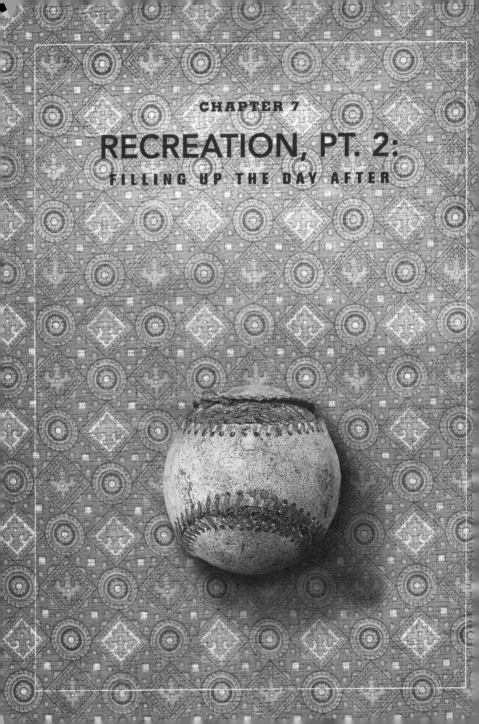

CHAPTER 7

RECREATION, PT. 2:

FILLING UP THE DAY AFTER

FUN & GAMES

(AFTER SOMEONE LOSES AN EYE)

The weekend. It has taken on an almost-sacred quality in Western life. For two of our major religions, 50% of it is literally sacred. And the secular world is swiftly catching up. Americans will take any pretext to expand it to three, even four days. Europeans increasingly start theirs at about 4pm every weekday.

So much do we value this idyllic stretch of game-watching, beer-drinking, errand-doing, and casual-sex-seeking that many would openly declare (sing, even) that their lives are dedicated to "working for" it.

Well cheer up, many. All that work is about to pay off. Our current pace of frenetic industrialization, development, and competition is soon going to lead us—one way or another—to a state that can only be described as "The Permanent Weekend."

It's hard to believe John Lennon didn't include the lyric "Imagine there's no Mondays," but no matter. He wouldn't have to lived to see it come true. But play your cards right, and you just might. On the **Apocalendar** there is no Monday, or Thursday, or for that matter, First Day of School, Tax Day, Arbor Day or any other singularly hated day.[55]

If you make it through the tumult, you will literally have all the time in the world (or at least what's left of it). Will you make the most of it? Just because the majority of habitable land has gone to waste doesn't mean your time has to! Get off your butt and seize the day—preferably, before someone seizes you.

---

[55] Why Arbor Day? All we're going to say is, it knows what it did.

10 THINGS TO DO BEFORE THE REST OF HUMANITY DIES

✔ 1. Sightsee

2. Learn a Foreign Language

3. Garden

4. Finally Write That Novel/Screenplay/Concept Album

5. Spend More Time with Your Family

6. Seek Out Old Loves

7. Take a Class

8. Stop Smoking/Drinking/Drugging

9. Catch Up on Your Reading

10. Volunteer

1. Always wanted to see the Grand Canyon? The majestic ruins of Athens? A glorious sunset from Maui's Mt. Haleakala? Travel might be difficult in this new era, but soon massive ruins, giant gashes in the ground, and sunset diffracted through layers of volcanic ash will be close at hand!

2. No matter which countries and races endure, the overall number of languages is going to dwindle, making it easier than ever to choose. And don't worry if it's difficult: what foreign-language speaker is going to quibble over your use of *tu* or *vous* when *vous* are the one sitting on the petrol reserve?

3. It used to be just for homemakers and retirees, but now that everyone's retired (and likely had to make their own home), this famously relaxing pastime is as close as the patch of land you also call "the bathroom." Plus, no more fretting over weeds—they're a key part of your diet now.

4. No deadlines, no rejection letters, no meddling editors or producers, no critics, and best of all, no philistine public! Imagine the freedom of being able to create whatever you want and enjoy the exact same crushing wave of indifference as if you'd done it commercially.

5. Odds are you will not survive the apocalypse with as many family members as you had before. Ergo: more time for each. Not to mention, in this new world, you can pretty much decide afresh who is and isn't in your family. Bye-bye, unemployed, alcoholic brother-in-law, hello Strong-Guy-with-all-the-Guns!

6. Still pining for an ex or an old crush, or just wondering whether you'd have had a shot with someone if things had gone differently? Well, guess what: they've gone *spectacularly* differently now.

7 Admittedly, the offerings will be slimmer, the facilities less desirable, and the faculty of more questionable accreditation. But if you can find anyone anywhere willing to teach anything, get ready for an unprecedentedly low student-teacher ratio and a true "free-for-all" atmosphere.

8. If any of these substances are still around and you have access to them, chances are they're better used for currency/bribes/surgical anesthesia. (For substitutes, see Ch. 6: *Sex, Drugs, & Rocks*.)

9. That intimidating pile of *New Yorkers* you never got around to—probably wiped out. And as for those thick biographies, historical surveys, or ambitious novels? If their size is still too daunting, feel free to do some vigorous "editing."

10. Whether it's serving gruel to the caveless or teaching a child to read fragments of text from a burned-out civilization, you can make a difference. Best of all, you can do as much or little as you want, without the burdensome pressure of having to "save the world."

POSTWAR GAMES

Any way you look at it, people around the world devote an inordinate amount of their time to sports—whether in the form of live play; practice or attendance; broadcast-enjoying; electronic and print news coverage; barside argumentation; or conversation with those we have no common interests with or affection for.

The only problem is, occasionally we have to curtail or suspend our steady diet of sports consumption because of inconveniences like "work" or "obligations" or "children."

But when the rules change and the old structures melt away, get ready for something the talk radio stations only pretend to promise:

ALL SPORTS, ALL THE TIME.

In some ways, too, the very nature of the most popular sports is bound to change. Rather than launch into a detailed discussion of how various end-of-world scenarios would impact each game, we present such changes in the only form comprehensible to sports fans: a box score.

Of course, there will be some minor cosmetic changes to the games we know and love. For starters, **a number of common sports terms and idioms will have to be retired.** In light of the recent Cataclysm, they will have either lost their metaphorical impact or have way too much of one. Among them:

- BLITZ
- STRIKE
- SAFETY
- SACRIFICE
- DRIBBLING
- END ZONE
- LONG BOMB
- INJURY TIME
- "HOT CORNER"
- SUDDEN DEATH
- BODY CHECKING
- SHOOTING GUARD
- KILLING THE CLOCK
- PENALTY SHOOTOUT

	FOOTBALL	BASEBALL	BASKETBALL	SOCCER	HOCKEY	GOLF
NUCLEAR BOMB	Slower game due to lead helmets	Steroids lose their stigma in era of mutants	Nothing but net... and maybe a little fallout	Massive hair loss means lots more "heading"	Nuclear winter= year-round season!	Much easier to find lost, glowing ball
ALIEN INVASION	Wide receivers cultivated for their big, delicious shoulders	Premium "skybox" seats sold aboard Mothership	New penalty call: "Inter-Dimensional Travelling"	Goalies cultivated for their big, delicious thighs	New technology makes smashed teeth instantly replaceable	Sapping of entire water supply means no more water hazards!
NONHUMAN TAKEOVER	Best cheerleaders reserved for breeding stock	"Bobblehead Day" entails actual human heads.	Players can now be ejected for "putsch-talking"	Powerful overlords still unable to control enraged/ excited fans	You don't want to know what the puck is made of	You think humans look ridiculous in golf togs?
MAD GENIUS	"And the star of the Super Bowl Half Time Show: Morty the Malevolent! ...Again."	Infinite designated hitters, hatched from Morty's clone army	Ball at constant risk from specially trained "Uber-Bees"	Headbutting riskier for freshly resurrected zombie players	"Let's see your precious ice after I BLOW UP THE SUN!"	Average par increased due to rejiggering of terrestrial gravity
ASTEROID	"Crater" replaces "football field" as unit of measurement	Batter walks if hit with baseball or shard of red-hot rock	Five points for throwing basket from over freshly created Fault Line	Equatorial reorientation will make N. America champs, S.America indifferent	New Ice Age renders boundary lines obsolete	Extra challenge of putting around Triffids
ECOLOGICAL/ NATURAL CATASTROPHE	Extra-extra point for kicking ball through ozone hole	More games postponed for "Acid Rain Delay"	Tallest players taken for tree foraging	New game cheer: "Coooooold!!!!"	Game venue switched to still-cooling lava fields	Sand-based courses littered with "grass traps"
RAPTURE	Waterboys take on extra importance in new fiery conditions	Tie goes to whomever Christ decides, upon his return	Great opportunity for Christian slam dunks on the way up	"Red Card" means you're not just ejected from the game....	Cross-sticking becomes powerful new means of protection	Pestilence, Slaughter, Desolation, Death: the ultimate foursome
NEUTRON BOMB	No longer any such thing as "second string"	Only five people required to do "The Wave"	Players no longer distracted by incessant paternity suits	Greatly reduced chance of being trampled if your team loses	More challenging surface due to absence of Zamboni drivers	Never have to "play through" again
EPIDEMIC	Fewer tackles because pads now slathered with hand sanitizer	Pitchers encouraged to limit pre-throw "crotch touches"	Foul = coming within five yards of opponent	"No hands" rule now self-enforcing	Penalty Box = quarantine	Fans kept at distance, requiring louder "golf clap"

A League of Your Own ☢

In a less-populated world, you won't get shut out by such pre-pocalyptic divisions as "pro" vs. "amateur," "major-league" vs. "minor-league," or "athletic" vs. "all-four-limb-possessing." Want to get in the game? **It's as easy as six simple steps.**

❶ **Pick a sport,** using the Box Scores as your guide.

❷ **Team up**. Locate a bare minimum of able-bodied folk of all ages, sizes, and genders,[56] and congratulations! Everybody made the one-round draft pick.

❸ **Assign positions.** No more messy politics over who plays what. Now you can decide it the meritocratic way: based on who brings you the choicest items of tribute. BONUS: As the organizer operating with scarce manpower, you can make yourself coach, quarter-back/pitcher/forward, and head cheerleader all at once.

❹ **Find an arena.** Depending on the nature of the Catastrophe, any number of actual pro-fessional sports arenas may be left open—though you may find them disorienting. The cognitive dissonance of kicking off in Mastercard IBM Cheez-Whiz Field may be too much in a world now lacking all three. We recommend staking out a patch of non-irradi-ated or frozen-over land, and keeping it well and distinctly marked with daily territorial uri-nation.

❺ **Procure equipment.** Hopefully, some remnants of the original sport's accoutrements can be scavenged. Barring that, however, get creative! For football, inflate a real pigskin. An hour with black mud and white chalk can transform even the most angular skull into a soccer ball. And don't think of it as a petrified eyeball—now it's a pretty fine golf ball.

❻ **Name your team.** Under present-day laws, sports teams can only be named after one of four things:

    ① Synonyms for "fighting person" ("Give 'em hell, Pugilists!")

    ② Aggressive or temperamentally unpleasant creatures ("Touchdown! Vultures win! Vultures win!")

    ③ Strange abstract nouns ("Let's go, Gra-vity!" [*clap-clap, clapclapclap*])

    ④ Insulting terms for Native Americans ("Gooooo Scalpers!")

> But with the great annihilation of most if not all team logos, insignias and branded merchandise,[57] the naming field will be wide open. To help you get started, here are a few suggested names and mascots:

---

[56] Sorry, WNBA—your glory days are over.
[57] Except for Dodger Dogs, which are scientifically engineered to last 6,000 years.

MASCOT "Tardy Tom"

CHEER "Here we go, Stragglers, here we go… eventually!"

M "Double Felix"

C "P-E, R-P-E/T-U, A-T-E!/ Let's do it/ Let's do it!"

M "Mr. Mute"

C "M-U-T, A-T-E/Don't do it/Don't do it"

M "Hy Pothermia"

C "G-g-g-g-gimme an I-I-I-I–aw screw it!"

M "Carrie the Carrier"

C "Get a-way from me/ Get back/Get back!"

M "Ol' #3695"

C "Be–submissive! Be, be, submissive!"

LEISURE OF THE PACK

FUN FOR THE WHOLE CLAN

One of the biggest laments of the modern age is that families don't spend enough time doing things together. Kids complain of overworked and physically or emotionally absent parents, while parents complain they can't even get the kids to sit down to dinner. (Even on Chicken Night! I mean, come on–*chicken*.)

For these reasons, among others, sociologists, psychologists, politicians and values advocates worry that the institution of family is in mortal danger. But that's just stinking thinking. The good news–no, great news–is that soon will come a set of circumstances that will force families to spend huge amounts of time together. Whether it be radioactive fallout, red-hot volcanic ash, or roving packs of bionic aardvarks, the savior of the family is on its way–and likely to be scratching at the door.

And whether you're actually holed up with your biological family or those you've newly designated as such, you're not just going to have time to kill – you're going to have time to *massacre*.

> Here is your arsenal of weapons.[61]

---

[61] Not to be confused with your actual arsenal of weapons, which admittedly take on less of a "leisurely" feel.

CARD GAMES

- *War*—Just like the traditional method, except, to reflect the current situation, winner physically beats the crap out of loser
- *Go Fish , But for God's Sake Don't Eat Them*—A game best played with gloves
- *Old Maid*—An old classic, whose name these days refers to an unmated 20-year-old woman
- *Gin Rummy*—Whoever ends up with the fewest cards wins—except in the sense that cards can now be traded for firewood
- *Poker*
  - *Two-Card Stud*—Best for situations of card scarcity and easier than ever to guess which cards are "in the hole" (the ones whose owners are)
  - *Territory Hold 'Em*—Variant where your betting strategy depends on your position—not around the table, in the social hierarchy (see Ch.8 for more on this).
  - *Strip*—Recommended for global warming/perpetual sunstorm situations—the loser is the winner!

KARAOKE

Karaoke has become a well-established way to bring collaborating strangers together through the unbreakable bond of ritual humiliation. Were you always too shy or self-conscious to reveal your shaky singing voice to others? Kiss that fear goodbye. Considering how rough the musical accompaniment is likely to be (a cool little two-rock, catgut-lyre and goatskin drum trio?), you're going to come out sounding like an angel.

CHARADES

What used to be an intellectual challenge of maddening difficulty ("*How* exactly do I pantomime 'Jumanji?'") is now a snap. Why? There's no movies. There's no TV shows. Except for the Boomboard 25, with the loss of electronic recordings, there will be vanishingly few songs in collective memory. That leaves pretty much books—and no one reads that many books anymore. The result? Around 50 things to guess from, max. Say goodbye to "Win, Lose, or Draw"—and hello to "Win, Win, or Win!"

COLLECTING

In an age when hoarding is one of the top survival skills, it's the collectors who will come out on top. Veteran philatelists and numismatists can finally acquire some of those rare stamps and coins that have eluded them, depending on how far they're willing to roam and how much rubble to dig through. Newbies can find all manner of functionally unusable but attractive curios to build a hobby around. Envision the pride of being able to invite a potential mate in to see your gleaming, expertly-curated "dialysis machine collection."

"VIRTUAL" VIDEO GAMES

Okay, obviously, you won't get to play them for real. But remember: they were only simulations of reality to begin with.

Besides, there's no reason their repetitive conflicts and situations can't be reenacted live. More to the point, video games at present are socially isolating and possibly brain-melting. By contrast, instead of cooping yourself up inside, pretending to steal cars or shoot down zombies, soon you'll be able to go outside and get sunlight and fresh air doing it for real.[62]

BOARD GAMES

There's really only one you need, a slight variation on a beloved classic heretofore to be known as

ARMAGEDONOPOLY

---

[62] Unless there's neither of those—but hey, it's still exercise.

GO! FAST!

SUBTERRANEAN AVE.

COMMUNITY HOARD

BALLISTIC AVE.

NCOMING ATTACKS

NUCLEAR

BURNEDWALK

DARK PLACE

ASTEROID

EXTREMELY SHORT LINE

PULVERIZER AIMED-AT-YOU

COMMUNITY RANSOM

MAD GENIUS

ARMAGED

ECOLOGICAL

GO TO QUARANTINE

STARVIN' GARDENS

ATLANTIC OVER-YOU

WATER DOESN'T WORK

CO₂ RAILROA

DOMESTIC LIFE & ENTERTAINING

In his play *No Exit*, Jean-Paul Sartre famously observed, "Hell is other people." If he's right (and he's been right about everything else), welcome to Heaven.

However, despite humanity's best efforts, the job will be incomplete. There will still be people, whether grouped with you into new functional survival units, imprisoned with you under another species' watchful eye(s), or clashing with you over scarce resources. How do you deal with them? Here as in so many other cases, **there are exactly only two options:**

Option A
Crush them mercilessly, driving them before you with great weeping and gnashing of teeth, and drinking the blood of victory directly from their vanquished skulls.[63]

Option B
If you can't beat 'em, *charm 'em.*

Invite the "new neighbors" over for a meal, an evening, or if you're particularly ambitious, a festive shindig. By mastering just a few tricks of the trade, in no time you'll have your guests partying like it's what-we-feared-would-happen-in-1999.

[63] Not recommended if your pre-pocalyptic doctor prescribed a low-sodium diet.

Decorating We recommend designing your affair around a theme. Some popular choices might include: "Perpetual Winter Wonderland," "Enchantment Under the Earth," or simply "Looks Like We Made It." You might also plan around one of the many Brand-New-World Holidays:

Christmukkwanzadan—The long-awaited strategic merger of winter holidays that everyone left can celebrate.

Neo-Thanksgiving—Closer than ever to the spirit—and conditions—of the first one, just without all that decadent "maize."

Helloween—Who can fail to be moved by the sight of kids, decked out in festive ash and burlap, going from home to home asking for bone meal?

Desistence-from-Labor Day—In a complete reversal, now the one day a year not observed by grilling animal flesh outside.

Saiparrickday—Although its origins are hazy, its small core of practitioners have carried on its traditions of wearing green and intoxication.

Invitations Gone is the pressure of buying fancy stationery or giving people six weeks' advance notice. Carve a note in any public place, and your job is done. Just make sure to include key guest information like location, sun's position in the sky, attire (ex: Scavenging Casual, Loin Cloth Optional), and, if you'd like, BYOB (Bring Your Own Beasts).

Food & Drink While many things will change culinarily about the world to come, one that will not is party foods. Sushi is just as popular (small portions don't fill you up or with radiation), as are party staples like finger foods and pigs in a blanket, only now in literal form.

Icebreakers If something drastic has happened to the Earth's axis, orbit, or atmosphere, you may actually have to break ice in order to get the party started. Otherwise, it's always a good idea to start with topics of common interest: "Barely tolerable weather we're having, eh?" "How 'bout those hyenas?" "Anyone here managed to reach groundwater?"

Activities Stick to the classics: everyone loves a good barter, and there's never a bad time to promote anonymous mating. Just remember to pay attention to your guests' level of interest. If they're starting to nod off, maybe it's time to cool it with the family vacation cave-drawings.

If You Are Invited… Be a considerate guest. Pick something nice from your stash to bring over, show up on time (or at least within the 15-hour window most parties will occupy), and make sure to compliment the host or hostess. (A simple "You're looking fat" will take you a long way.) If possible, try and send a "thank-you slave" within two weeks of the event.

BEFORE WE BLOW

It may not seem like there's much you can do now to entertain yourself later, but remember: one of the most beloved activities in an era without recorded media will be the oral recollection of movies, TV shows, and plays seen now. To that end, we recommend you:

• Prioritize your TV and movie consumption into "Must-See", "Could-See", and "Will See Only If I Have to, Like on a Date."

• Start collecting books that serve one of two functions: a) useful survival info, or b) timekiller/firestarter.

Some suggestions:
- *Robinson Crusoe*
- *Absolute Worst Case Scenarios*
- *Oxford English Dictionary: Extremely Unabridged Edition*
- anything by James Michener

CHAPTER 8

CAREER, WEALTH
& POWER

DON'T JUST SURVIVE...
THRIVE!

Strange as it may sound, there will be those for whom the permanent weekend will eventually get old. The go-getters, the entrepreneurs, those whom we call "Type-A Personalities," but in the soon-to-be reduced human population, will simply be known as "Personalities."

In fact, if you're reading this book in pre-apocalyptic times, that shows you have foresight and plan ahead—so you just might be one of them. Man, do we hate people like you.[64]

But if the Big Day(s) has already happened, and you've found this in the rubble, stolen it, or bartered/murdered[65] for it, congratulations! You just survived the largest downsizing in human history.

So what are you waiting for? Drag yourself out, up, through, or whatever preposition you're hiding behind and take a look at the world around you. What do you see? In all likelihood, decimated structures, smoking ruins, and vast stretches of desolate or ravaged land that used to teem with people.

In other words: THE BEST JOB MARKET EVER.

---

[64] Except for your book-buying habits, of course.
[65] "Barter-Murder-One": a common post-apocalyptic misdemeanor

☐ **NOTHING BUT VACANCIES**

Not just for jobs (although pretty much any free-standing structure or institution might as well have an "Inquire Within" sign hanging on it)—in general. You can choose to live wherever you want, and have a five-step commute to work.

☐ EASY INTERVIEWS

Here are some words you will never *ever* hear again:

"Underqualified"

"Overqualified"

"Yes, but *how well* do you know Excel?"

"We're really looking for someone with specific experience in _____."

"Mandatory urine test"

Here are some words you can expect to hear a lot:

"Do you have your own hair? You're hired."

☐ SOCIAL MOBILITY

No longer just an abstract concept touted by the upper class to feel less guilty about their successful transition to the upper-upper-class. In the coming days, expect to see everyone on the move, professionally and geographically.

☐ JOB STABILITY

You can breathe easy (metaphorically), knowing your job is just as secure as anything else around you.

☐ GREAT HOURS

With artificial lighting hard to come by, don't expect to be pulling too many late nights. The midnight oil itself is too costly.

☐ SALARY & BENEFITS

Ever wish you could name your own salary? Now you can, especially as your salary is likely to be in the form of livestock. Want health care? You're certain to be getting the best available. And when it comes to pensions, rest assured. The retirement funds are just as secure and reliable as those of any company operating today.

☐ BE YOUR OWN BOSS

It's just simple numbers, really. You'll probably also get to be your own secretary, receptionist, VP of Sales, and temp.

No doubt about it, the end times will be nothing short of an employees' market. The only question is: Which job is right for you?

APOCALYPTIC APTITUDE TEST

I would characterize my working style as _____.

   A. slow and steady

   B. procrastination, combined with bursts of efficiency

   C. well-armed

My co-workers would describe me as the office _____.

   A. workaholic

   B. clown

   C. hunter-gatherer

I prefer to work on projects that are _____.

   A. long-term and in-depth

   B. short-term and always-changing

   C. underground

The most important aspect of a job to me is _____.

   A. salary

   B. creative satisfaction

   C. creative salary

In five years, I see myself _____.

   A. in a senior management or executive position

   B. owning my own business

   C. in someone else's belly

KEY: Score 1 point for each answer of "a," 5 points for each "b," and 10 for each "c."

- 1-12: You are a hardworking, stability-loving, "nose to the grindstone" type. Fortunately for you, there will be plenty of jobs in that precise field.

- 13-36: You value work and leisure in equal proportions. You would do best to seek out part-time work--(ie: work only during the times that it's safe to be outside).

- 37-50: You are ideally suited to any profession the afterworld has to offer and will be immediately snapped up by employers (if not giant tarantulas).

HE FASTEST-GROWING EMPLOYMENT SECTORS

bitary Lawyer

You thought the law was confusing and impenetrable now, wait until the definition of jurisdiction is "the owning of a rifle." Are you fleet of tongue and fleeter of foot? Slap a billboard on a passing wagon, and you're in business.

Management Consultant

Every hastily formed social unit is going to have its kinks, and someone needs to help iron them out. Much like their contemporary counterparts, these indispensable advice-mongers will need no experience and get to travel from site to site, recommending who's to be terminated.

Eventual Responder

"Where's the fire?" *Everywhere*. So what's the hurry? It's not like there's a hospital to rush anyone to. The perfect vocation for those who like to help *and* relax.

155

THE FASTEST-GROWING EMPLOYMENT SECTOR
(CONT

Sales + Marketing

A profession where the jargon of old really comes to life in the afterworld. Where all you need is fire and a piece of metal to take advantage of "branding opportunities," and you can "capture market share" with nothing more than a nighttime raiding party. And best of all, *no more cold calls!*

COWBOY

As a child, you only dreamed that this was a viable career option. Now it's the only way to go for those who, for one reason or another, need to go. Another childhood-fantasy job now available is *Astronaut*— only now, you get to walk on an unrecognizable, oxygen-deprived, pock-marked planet without all those boring, crunchy-ice-cream-eating, diaper-wearing months in transit!

Involuntary

The primary economic engine in the event of a nonhuman takeover. Possibly the job field with the widest range: one day you might be chained to others in a barrel, stomping the mash that will become banana liqueur; the next day, bathing His Amphibious Majesty.

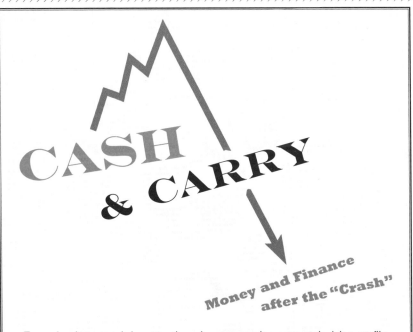

CASH & CARRY

Money and Finance after the "Crash"

Every day, it seems, brings another glossy magazine cover, television profile, or glowing biography of one of the world's multi-billionaires, shimmering princes who apparently exist only on yachts or at exclusive ski resorts. Every item that greets them from morning til night is covered in gold, and champagne is like water to them. And don't even get us started on the gold champagne.

How many times have you looked upon such people and thought, *Wow, I wish I could be like him.*

Or, alternately, *Wow, I wish he would lose all his riches in a sudden, earth-melting cataclysm.*

Friend, sometimes 50% of wishes do come true.

And while you're not exactly going to crawl out of the rubble and into a diamond-encrusted stretch Humvee,[66] you will soon have the opportunity to become *one of the richest people on Earth.*

It all begins with the world ending.

---

[66] The gas consumption of which may have, in fact, helped precipitate the rubble.

Oh yes, and

The Apocalypse How Three-Step, 100% Satisfaction-Guaranteed-or-Your-Money-Back,[67] Wealth-Building Program Plan.

Step 1:
Inventory

Much like Alcoholics Anonymous participants are instructed to make a "searching and fearless inventory" of themselves, you'll need to do the same to determine your total assets: searching, without getting scared off by rival "assessors." Also like AA participants, in doing so, you are quite likely to fall off a wagon.

But how do you assess the value of what you have? Here at the Apocalypse How Think Tank (the only one around with armor and actual firepower), our Apocalyptonomists have come up with a symbolic currency equivalent, the Armageddollar ($A).

To determine what your loot is worth in $, simply cut out and carry around this handy *Pouch-Sized Conversion Guide:*

---

[67] Just mail the book (or at least this section of it) back to us at: *Apocalypse How*
2012 Bygone Lane
And wait for a dreary Postman, making one last round while   Truth or Consequences, Newer Mexico
witnessing the world die, to deliver your refund.   Underneath U.S.A

Cataclysmic Conversions

USE	Value ($A)
Construction	25
Repair	10
Transportation	35
Protection	
- Weather	12
- Human Adversaries	20
- Armies of	
- The undead	9
- Giant mutant creatures	6
- Killing machines	17
Surgery	35
- Major	20
- Elective	50
- Impromptu	25
Food	15
Drink	
Food Preparation	
- Crushing/Chopping	8
- Mixing	6
- Heating	13
- Detoxifying	20

CONVENIENCE	
Portable	9
Hideable	12
Replaceable	-8
Throwable	14

INTANGIBLE VALUE	
Cultural	8
Nostalgic	13
Religious	
- Armageddon-Era	5-10
- Pre-Armageddon	.25

Increasing Your Inventory:
Three Surefire Methods

1. Beg

Admittedly, it'll be tough to get sympathy in this harsh new environment ("Oh, you've still got one leg? Lucky bastard.") But it's not impossible. You just need to be creative. Think of new causes for pity ("I am atrocious at time management"), dream up more contemporary versions of old sign offers ("Will Not-Infect for Food"), or busk with musical selections likely to stir a survivor's heart ("Hey, Mister, wanna hear the theme song from 'Friends'?")

2. Borrow

Gone are the restrictive formalities of olden times, where you had to "be close to" or "know" or "have ever spoken to" a neighbor before asking to borrow a tool or supply. These days, the honest, old-fashioned fear of having one's habitations set on fire is ample incentive for a) him to lend you that sharp-rock-tied-to-a-stick, or cup of gravel; and b) you to give it back.

3. Steal

…unless you have, like, a motorcycle.

Real Estate:
Collateral, Damaged

You may be overlooking one of the prime assets of the afterworld: your property. Depending on where you've ended up, you just might be sitting on gold.

ASK YOURSELF THE FOLLOWING QUESTIONS:

Am I sitting on gold?

One of the best places to take refuge from any conflagration is an old abandoned mine shaft. Do some digging around and see what color mineral gets under your fingernails. Even if you're just sitting on coal, that can be a vital heat and power resource. Less certain in value would be taking refuge in an old abandoned chalk mine.[68]

Do I maintain armed control of my own home?

As mentioned in Chapter 2, the first few days and weeks after the apocalypse are going to be a "squatters' market." However, once the initial period of settling and entrenchment ends, hordes of speculators will hit the road, seeking better quarters (for some reason, still mostly on Sundays). Consider renting out your digs for added income. Or if you're looking to move on yourself, remove the provisional walls you've thrown up on one side and hold an "Open Shelter."

> **Helpful Hint:** If you know potential buyers are coming over, bake something fragrant in whatever you're using for an oven. We recommend piping-hot, gooey "cinnamon rodents."

Can I make this a multiple-use property?

Certainly the afterworld will have its share of zones: radioactive, contagious, demilitarized, extra-militarized. But when it comes to property zoning, there will be nothing of the sort! You can turn your one-room lean-to into a combination trading post/mongrel slave brothel/shrine/pay toilet, and the only obstacles you'll face will be olfactory.

---

[68] Unless the earth has been taken over by a gruff-but-dedicated principal from an alien species, whose complete destruction of the planet is just part of a tough-love attempt to give humanity the self-esteem we need to escape from our poor, ghetto planet through the power of education.

Step 2:
Leverage

If You Got It, Gouge It!

Increasing your net assets—defined generally as whatever assets you've managed to swoop up in a net—is really just a matter of simple economics. Here is the conventional supply-and-demand graph:

Under pre-apocalyptic norms, when demand increases, price goes up, motivating producers to increase quantity, which then meets the pent-up demand, lowering the price. The point where both curves meet in the middle is the ideal price that maximizes sales and revenue.

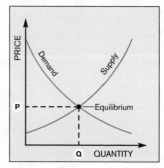

However, according to Apocalyptonomics:

If you control the supply, you can charge whatever the hell you want—until a demand is made at the business end of a rifle, spear, or Alpha Centauran *blaglorpf*. [69]

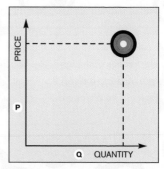

---

[69] Which, if you've ever had one pointed at you, is enough to make you think twice about laughing at its owner's "ass-tentacles."

Comparison Swapping

The one thing there will not be a shortage of in the end times is opportunities to barter. Indeed, huge swathes of land that once contained shopping malls will now be covered in wares as far as the eye can see. Imagine going to the mall without having to find parking or difficult-to-locate stores, and with dining options just as appetizing and healthy as before. The only difference is that the Food Court will actually be empowered to conduct trials and carry out executions.

But if you want to increase your personal worth, don't just grab whatever you have around and go on a swapping spree. A little planning and a few pointers will elevate your social status from "bagman" to "multi-bagman."

Size matters

The bigger and heavier the item, the more willing its owner is to part with it. Drive home this point by pretending to groan with effort as you attempt to lift it, dissuading him/her from wanting to pack it back up, and fellow swappers from wanting it at all. If you were an actor or theater major, finally—a chance to make that yield financial rewards!

Use your contagion

Radioactive? Contaminated? Infectious? Simply touch (or better, cough or bleed on) the item of your choice, and it's as good as yours.

Invoke the competition

"I've seen it selling for only *two* water-purification tables at So-and-So's barter" can work surprisingly well. What are they going to do, phone up So-and-So and ask for a price check?

Play down interest

Current conditions provide you any number of pretexts to disavow interest (thereby decreasing the price). Some sample ones: "Well, I might be captured and enslaved." "Hmm, I might not make it til morning." "Ooh yeah, I'm kinda on the run from fire-breathing wolves. . . ."

And if all else fails...

Don't be afraid to walk/stagger/limp away.

Seriously—the post-apocalypse is one time when the swapper has most reason to doubt they'll ever see you again. If they don't make a deal now, they never will.

Step 3: Invest

You've seen it before, if not in person then on TV or depicted in movies: the trading floor of the New York Stock Exchange, or any of America's or the world's exchanges. Vicious, frenzied places where "greed is good," and grown men and women shout, clamor, and claw for every ounce of possible gain.

Now imagine getting to take part in that, but *without having to wear a suit*.

In this new environment, anyone can make a killing. But if you want to make the financial kind, forget everything you learned before "Black Tuesday" (and Wednesday, Thursday, Friday...) and follow these **Principles of Apocalyptic Investing:**

Buy High, Sell Low

The new world will be divided into two main groups: those living aboveground and those not. The former will have access to a wider variety of goods old, new, refurbished, and creatively repurposed,[70] while those cowering below will have to make do with what they've hoarded. The profit opportunity for you is obvious— gather your best loot and start searching for airholes.

---

[70] You will never truly appreciate human ingenuity until you've seen a "beer helmet" turned into an IV drip.

Time the Market

It's often been said that the current investment market operates according to a "mob mentality." But soon, you'll actually have the chance to observe the mob forming, lighting their torches, and stampeding. If Frankenstein's monster had been in such a position, he might have said, "Apocalypse…Friend."

Unify Your Portfolio

In a topsy-turvy world of scattered goods and resources, everyone's going to have a hodgepodge. The only way to stand out is to specialize. You want customers to come to you because they've heard far and wide about "The Canned-Peas Guy."

So what exactly should you be investing your money (or analogue thereof) in? Here are a few tips for the wise investor:

Biotech

Get in on this early. Everyone's going to want a piece of cutting-edge experimental lab science once they see all the living examples of it walking around.

Luxury Goods

A solid growth opportunity, because the definition will keep shifting to include whatever functional, well-constructed pre-apocalyptic items are left. Today's Radio Flyers are the Rolls-Royces of tomorrow.

Municipal Bonds

As long as we're talking about the kind that self-appointed law enforcement officers will use to tie the hands of lawbreakers, this is a product with endless growth. Same thing goes for stocks of the public, wooden, neck-holding variety.

Utilities

Forget about it. If they're up and running, they're under the control of some-one else (quite possibly, the computers we built to run them). If not, as soon as word gets out that you have running water, electricity, or natural gas, your organs are going to end up in the hands of some "inside traders."

Plastics

Still sound advice, even long after *The Graduate* can no longer be seen on working equipment. But not the companies manufacturing it, only usable items made of it: whether we're talking bottles, jugs, baggies, legs, or action figures, this non-biodegradable wonderstuff is good as gold, if not better. Why? Because if all else fails, the smell of it burning is enough to repel even the hardiest "corporate raiders."[71]

Retail

A can't-miss sector, since in the "days after," the "made-to-order" sector is likely to nosedive.

So that's the <u>Apocalypse</u> <u>How</u> financial program. Follow those three steps, and you're on your way to making it into the elite ranks of the Fortune 5!

[71] Versus: When's the last time you wrinkled your nose and said, "Ew, what's that? Gold?"

Power, Position, & Politics:

Making It to the Top of the Rubble

Throughout human history, we have spent an inordinate amount of time, energy, and resources jockeying for primacy, constantly searching for advantage and weakness, each one of us trying our damnedest to be "King of the Mountain."

But stop for a moment and "do the aftermath." On a planet likely to contain not many more people than mountains, just about everyone can be King of one.

Of course, as the old saying goes, "It's lonely at the top." But let's not kid ourselves: it's going to be lonely anyway. You might as well enjoy the view.

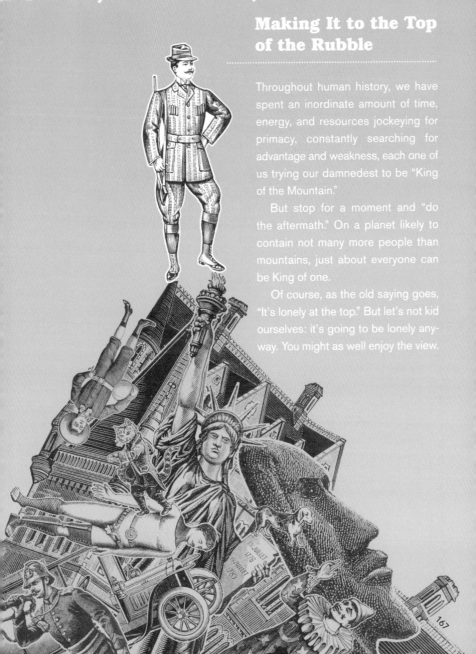

167

 POST-CATASTROPHIC POLITICS:

A PRIMER

★ ★ ★

"Too much money in politics."
"No true representation of my interests."
"A crazy dictator who jails us for listening to 'decadent' music."

Wherever they live, people today are almost all frustrated with their system of governance. Fortunately, the apocalypse will change all that. All the tired old political labels and practices will be erased from memory like undesirable electronic votes. It's a heady time of political re-invention, comparable to the early days of the American Revolution—only with fewer poofy wigs, and a greater chance of dying from smallpox.

Just how much power and influence can you wield over your fellow non-fatalities? In part, it depends on what type of political system they eventually organize themselves into.

Here are a few possible power structures that may come into play:

FOOD CHAIN

Used to be, we were safely ensconced at the top of this. But with severely reduced offerings on "Nature's Buffet," our world's power dynamics increasingly take on the form of "Doug eat Doug."

Leaders: The lean and hairy

Subjects: The slow and succulent

Lawmaking Body: Three chambers (Appetizers, Entrees, Inter-Legislative Snacks)

Governing Document: *To Serve Man*

Strategies for Success: Learn to run faster, bathe in urine

FEMOCRACY

Sisters—doing it of themselves, by themselves, and for themselves.

Leaders: Mean girls and prom queens

Subjects: Shrinking violets, non-naughty librarians, wallflowers, plain janes... oh yeah, and men

Lawmaking Body: The Gal-Pal-iament, a semi-secretive body of whispered caucuses and innuendoes, whose members are not formally voted in or out, but somehow *just know it*

Governing Document: Varies from month to month, depending on what the Document Club is currently reading

Strategies for Success: If you don't have a vagina, acquire one. If you do but still lack power, grow a pair (of breasts).

PECKING ORDER

The political system of choice for generations of poultry—and just look how far it's gotten them.

Leaders: "Sharp-beaked" races (Mediterranean, Semitic, pre-op Angeleno)

Subjects: The easily bruisable

Lawmaking Body: Open-air forum known as "The Yard"

Governing Document: *Chicken Little*

Strategies for Success: Put your nose to the grindstone.

CULT

No doubt about it—the political system with the most personality.

Leader: The first guy to think of this

Subjects: Everyone else, particularly men with hot wives/girlfriends

Lawmaking Body: The Leader's brief periods of lucidity

Governing Document: "Document? Reading makes His Holiness cry and take his Magic Pills!"

Strategies for Success: a) Be the Leader, b) Have a hot wife/girlfriend, c) Start a break-away faction.

ALPHABETICAL ORDER

Sometimes it's the simplest ideas that make the most sense.

Leaders: Alice-Mikey

Subjects: Neil-Zoe

Lawmaking Body: Surprising twist on established parliamentary procedure. For the first time ever, it's the A-H's that have it, not the I's.

Governing Document: *Merriam-Webster's Third New International Dictionary, Abridged*

Strategies for Success: A legally recognized name change is as easy as a trip to a judge, or alphabetically better yet, a barrister.

It is also entirely possible that none of these systems will take effect, and that you—through some combination of audacity, pluck, charisma, and (just guessing here) ammunition—will seize exclusive control of the humans in your vicinity. If so, you might do well to abide by…

The Seven Habits Of Highly Effective Petty Tyrants

1. Keep your friends close, but your enemies in barbwire-ringed holes in the ground.

2. Be ruthless, but sometimes also be ruthful.

3. It is better to be feared than loved, but better still is being "loved to be feared."

4. Always project strength, using shadow puppetry if necessary.

5. Do not show your face too much, especially if it is gargoyle-ugly.

6. Be swift with justice, swifter with mercy, and swiftest with intoxicants.

7. Power corrupts, but absolute power is absolutely awesome!

Historical Me-Visionism:

YOUR PATH TO IMMORTALITY

The march of human history is a long, immeasurably complex saga, full of documents, antiquities, and endless reams of media. For any person of the 21st century, it's an almost unbearable burden to shoulder.

So just think what a relief it will be to have most, if not all of it wiped out.

No more having to keep the Battle of Gettysburg straight from the Treaty of Hapsburg, the Norman Conquest from the Normandy Invasion, the Bronze Age from Zbigniew Brzezinski.

From the day after on, you're officially an "A+ Student of History," because you're rewriting it… to your advantage!

To quote George Santayana: "Those who forget the past are condemned to just believe whatever I say it is."[72]

Use the examples in the following chart as a guide, and start putting the "me" back into "history".

Old History	*Me-Vised History*
In 1215, the Magna Carta was issued by King John, establishing the basis for constitutional rule.	In 2005, Don King gave me the Magnet Card, establishing the basis for me ruling over you.
The Roman Empire, ruled by a series of Caesars, had a huge impact on the world of today, giving us everything from aqueducts to law codes.	Romania—the land we're living in today—was founded by Cesar Chavez and given to Aquaman, my father-in-law.
Until their mysterious collapse in the 9th century CE, most of Central America belonged to the Mayans.	America? Mine mine mine!
In the 16th century, the Protestant Reformation created a massive rift among Christians, prompting centuries of war.	Hey, remember the Christians? Whatever happened to those guys?

[72] Did he really say that? He did now!

CONQUER

RACISM. SEXISM. RELIGIOUS STRIFE. INTER-CLASS WARFARE.

All scourges of the current era, but not necessarily of the coming one. Rather, you can expect a grand sweeping away of the old prejudices—making room to invent brand new ones of your own!

Now social divisions aren't just a desirable end in themselves—they can also be useful in consolidating and elevating your position. Be one of the brains behind the new definitions of "us and them," and you've just signed up for elite membership in "Club Us."

RU

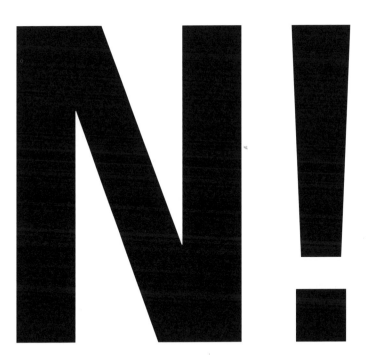

CONCLUSION

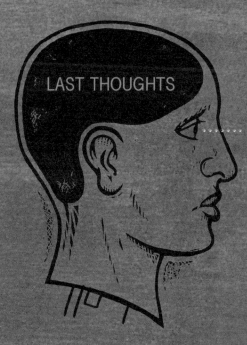

LAST THOUGHTS ...... EVER

SO NOW WHAT?

You know how to eat, hide, dress, socialize, date, play, work, work out, and party like an apocalyptic professional.

And yet, somehow, the sight of bleached human skulls scattered across a smoldering desert extending all the way to the dark purple cloud layer where the horizon used to be…is still occasionally a bit of a buzzkill.

Here's a few tips to brighten your day after . . .

Step 1: The Future is Now.

This is it. The end of the line. The last stop. You will never again have to plan, wait, or defer grat-ification for anything. Dig into the all-you-can-eat-*now* buffet that is your new, consequence-free existence. Hell, while you're at it, rip off the sneeze guard. You've survived world-shattering tribulations—you're not about to be felled by a case of the sniffles.

Even better, you won't—or should I say, *don't*—need to use the future tense anymore. Ever. So sit back, relax, and enjoy the luxury of using only 66% of your speech.

Step 2: It's Just an A-pocalypse, not THE-pocalypse.

That being said, who knows what wondrous surprises our cataclysm might have inciden-tally unleashed? Just because an asteroid collision reversed the earth's poles doesn't mean our vast arsenals of nuclear weapons couldn't *also* be set off by the electromagnetic frenzy. What if the aliens get cold tentacles and depart in the middle of the night, leaving our planet parched, decimated, and just a little bit lonelier?

Besides, just because the history of our species is ending doesn't mean another's might not be just beginning. And that could be to your advantage. Say you were a slob in your pre-catastrophic life, with an apartment that was always welcome to cockroaches. If they rise to the top of the new evolutionary heap, don't think your kindness will go unnoticed.

The point is, don't get bummed out by the world-ending hand you've been dealt. The universe has a funny way of shuffling the deck. In just a matter of hours, the pair of twos you're holding could be transformed into a full house (most likely, of refugees.)

Step 3: Stop and Smell the Corpses

Not literally, of course. That would provoke a response of—depending on your specific circumstances—either "Ew!" or "Back off! I called dibs!"

Rather, what we mean here is that you now have infinite time to kick back and appreciate that which is no longer. The choices are practically unlimited: buildings, institutions, great works of landscaping, particularly cunning highway off-ramps, scientific milestones, fields of scholarship, indelible advertising jingles, world records, flora, fauna, etc.

Don't mourn, don't wax nostalgic, certainly don't create an entire religious cult around the artifacts and comically misunderstood attributes of something long gone.

Instead, just try to savor all the accomplishments of our species that you took for granted when they were still functioning. If you're having trouble, here are some suggested "savoring points":

"How did we even think of that?"

"How did that work?"

"Remind me: what was that again?"

"Hey you! Get away from my thing!"

THIS, TRULY, IS THE ULTIMATE, TWO-PRONGED GIFT OF THE APOCALYPSE:

TO THOSE LIVING BEFORE IT, THE COMFORTING KNOWLEDGE THAT YOU CAN POSTPONE ALL YOUR GRATITUDE FOR EVERYTHING IN OUR LIVES UNTIL AFTER THE BIG ONE HITS. THAT FREES YOU UP TO FILL THE REMAINDER OF YOUR DAYS WITH THE GREATEST DELIGHT EVER KNOWN TO MAN:

AND TO THOSE WHO SURVIVE, IN THE WORDS OF JONI MITCHELL: "YOU DON'T KNOW WHAT YOU GOT TILL IT'S GONE." WE AS A SPECIES WILL SIMPLY HAVE NO GREATER OPPORTUNITY TO APPRECIATE JUST HOW MUCH WE HAD UNTIL IT'S ALL GONE.

THE PARKING LOT'S JUST BEEN UNPAVED, FOLKS. NOW GET OUT THERE AND REDISCOVER PARADISE!

EschatologuE

MOBILE ALTAR

Whether it's rain you want, favorable toxic winds (ie: away from you), or just general appeasement of the angry gods, this sturdy, lightweight, easy-to-assemble altar makes sacrifice a snap. Folds into a portable unit the size of a suitcase—perfect for those who are pious, terrified, and "on the go."

FEATURES:

- Adjustable "victim grooves" can accommodate everything from grain to goats to Grandpa.
- Do-it-yourself "icon window" allows altar to be customized for any religion, established or invented.
- Unique non-stick surface makes blood stains washable by means of water, sand, or (recommended) more blood.
- Guaranteed propitious, or your devotion back!

LEADWEAR

Tired of peering into your crag and saying, "I have nothing to wear?"

The future of fashion is (almost) here! Finally, clothing you can truly wear anywhere and not have that "exposed" feeling. Versatile all-weather combinations protect you from stinging rain, merciless sun, and endless winter. Glow with style, not radiation!

FEATURES:

- Wrinkle-free design makes sudden evacuation (either kind) worry-free.
- 100% stone-washable, or by machines both sentient and non.
- Exclusive "non-breathable fabric" makes contamination a thing of the (extremely recent) past.
- Specially designed light weave guarantees you "will more or less feel like you're not wearing lead."

THE PEE-CYCLER

Tired of fighting off bandits on your way to the river, or dealing with pesky diminishing groundwater? In a world where water is scarce and convenience stores not so convenient, thirst doesn't have to be the enemy—thanks to the "personal soda fountain" in your pants. Welcome to urinary reconstitution... the way it was *meant to be*.

FEATURES:

- Fun "flavor-pak" includes Grape, Melonberry, Extreme Orange, and Radical Root Beer.
- Straws come in both "straight" and "crazy," and would be washable if you had water.
- Optional "superblast" nozzles make it a fun game for parched kids.
- Patented Comfort Catheter™ design ensures your genitals won't even know it's working!

UTILITY BELT

It seems like it happens every day (or at least it will very soon): you're out on your own, miles from "civilization," and realize you forgot the tool you need—and no remains of a former hardware store in sight! This low-riding, easy-wearing, all-holding belt is the ultimate accessory for the ultimate days.

FEATURES:

- Expandable loops hold everything from a lock pick to a gas-siphoning tube to an animal-gutter.
- Available in desert camo, ice camo, or glowing-green camo
- Easy-to-use "cinch-and-go" waistband will shrink to accommodate even the most shriveled stomach.
- Snaps on in a flash (atomic, biochemical, or electromagnetic).

CUFF COZY

Imprisonment and forced labor never felt so snuggly.

AVAILABLE IN: wool, cotton, ermine, pleather, pubic.

NOVELTY BREATH MASKS

If you can't bring a smile to your kids' faces, at least you can strap one on them. Funny for onlookers, too—everyone around you who doesn't have one will literally die laughing.

AVAILABLE IN: Clown, Monkey, Bugs Bunny, SpongeBob, Richard Nixon

THE ELECTRICYCLE

Why throw out all those electrical appliances or throw them at enemies, when you can still put them to use, in brief spurts? Imagine the luxury of being able to open a can with an *electric* opener after just 2 hours of pedaling. Or the old-fashioned pleasure of gathering round with the family (all pedaling furiously) to listen to the radio. Make a game out of guessing who it is who keeps broadcasting "Someone…anyone…."

FEATURES:

• Storage batteries, on the off chance you produce more energy than you need without cramping up.

• Extra-padded seats for even the boniest butts.

*Order Now and we'll throw in two (2) Forehead Saltbands (sweat your way to a better dinner!)

AMNES-TEE SHIRTS

Disarm your atttackers with cleverly worded casualwear that's not just stylish—it's a "mercy statement."

AVAILABLE DESIGNS:

• I'm With Saved ☛

• My Parents Were Infested With Lice, And All I Got Was This Lousy T-Shirt

• I ♥ Maniacal Geniuses

• Kiss Me—I'm Fertile!

• I'd Rather Be Foraging

APPENDIX B

1. Massage Chair

The perfect remedy after a long day of fleeing, digging, or bartering.

YOU WILL NEED:
- One (1) strip of cloth or fabric, your length and width
- Hay, grass, or hair (human may be easiest to remove from source)

Find an area of maximum geologic vibration—whether due to explosions, the constant earthquakes/volcanoes, or the relentless march of the Cyborg Infantry. Set up cloth along this region, stuffing the material underneath as padding. Lean back and feel that terrestrial trauma work its magic on your lumbar.

2. Margarita Maker

An indispensable tool for social cohesion, and a way to make every day feel like Friday (which, for all you know, it might be.)

YOU WILL NEED:
- One (1) container, of any size or shape, as long as it can be poured from
- Three (3) knives or blades
- One (1) belt or strap
- Rotary power source (fuel-powered, human, animal, or something in between)
- Fruit
- Ice (depending on the global situation, either very easy or nearly impossible to obtain. If the latter, the plus side is that fruit fermentation is faster than ever!)

Assemble as shown here, and let the slightly-less-bad times roll!

3. Widescreen "TV"

YOU WILL NEED:
- One (1) white or light-colored rectangular piece of material or clean(ish) surface
- One (1) independent light source: solar, fire-based, or bioluminescent family member
- 5-10 double or triple-jointed toes
- One (1) active imagination and knack for storytelling

Sit between light source and screen, using toes to shape, animate, and project all manner of wondrous tales. Unless you're, like, really more into sports or porn. That can work, too.

"Now this is one apocalypse I could get used to."

Eat This Book

Well, okay, not the whole book. But this page in particular? Completely edible, and a great source of protein, trace minerals, and so much more. Check it out:

Nutrition Facts

Serv. Size 1 page (5½″ x 7½″)
Servings: 1

Amount Per Serving

Calories 3   Calories From Fat 0

% Daily Value *

Total Fat 0g	0%
Saturated Fat 0g	0%
Cholesterol 0mg	0%
Sodium 170mg	14%
Potassium 80mg	1%
Total Carbohydrate 5g	1%
Dietary Fiber 1g	8%
Sugars 4g	
Protein 6g	

*Percent Daily Values are based on a post-apocalyptic 500 calorie diet. Your values may be higher or lower depending on your nomadism/captors' feeding regimen.

SERVING SUGGESTIONS:

Paperdelle–Tear page into strips, toss with sauce of your choice…and enjoy!

Papanini–Fold page in half, lightly grill…and enjoy!

Paperrito–Roll this page up into a tube (making sure to fold the bottom to keep the oxygen from leaking onto you)…and enjoy!

Paper Steak–Fold page into a cunning model of a steak…and, well, you know the drill!

THIS PAGE   DELICIOUSLY   LEFT BLANK

BONUS PAGE II
PAGE OF RAGE

Page of Rage

Perhaps your greatest need is not nourishment but self-defence. If you are
in desperate straits, this page can be used as a weapon in three ways:

1.

Ripped out and used to papercut your adversary until he/she/it begs for mercy.
Skill Level: Little to None

2.

Folded into a paper airplane, as shown below, aimed well,
and used to blind the bastard.
Skill Level: Moderate to High

3.

Folded into a paper airplane and aimed with a trajectory that blinds, then papercuts.
Skill Level: Awesome to Ninjalike

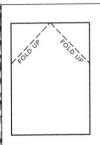 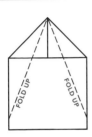  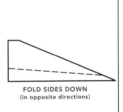

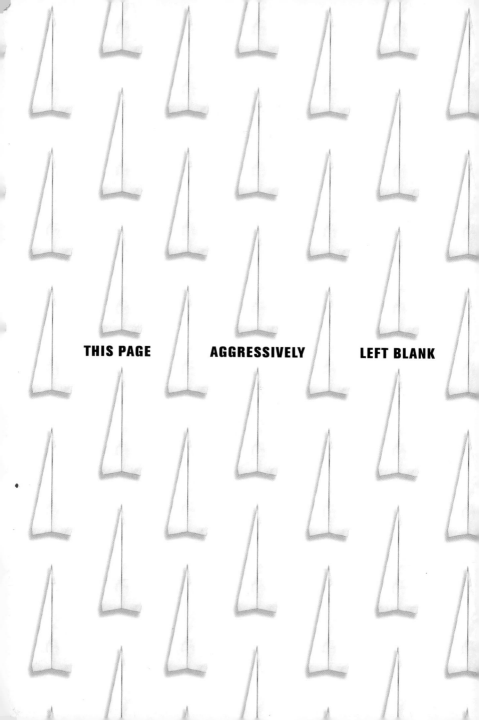

THIS PAGE   AGGRESSIVELY   LEFT BLANK

10 Seconds of Fire

Maybe you need to light a fire. Or see something really quick. Or make your dinner slightly less raw. Whatever your need, a little ignition, a little oxygen*, and now you're in business.

*Ignition and oxygen not included

THIS PAGE   COMBUSTIVELY   LEFT BLANK

PAGE OF SURRENDER

Page of Surrender

All else failed?

Rip out this page, attack to stick or protuberant device of your choosing, and *voila*–instant white flag.

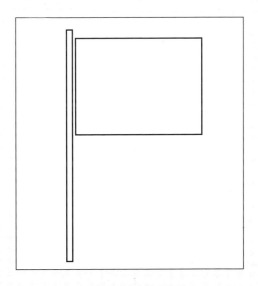

DOES IT REALLY MATTER WHAT THIS PAGE IS FOR?